Witty, Clever One Liners For All Occasions

The fourth classic collection of One Liners.

Companion to the three best-selling volumes:

4,000 One Liners

5,000 One Liners

Another 3,000 One Liners

by

Ray Prince

Published by Ray Prince

rprince@ozemail.com.au

ISBN: 978-0-9923849-5-1

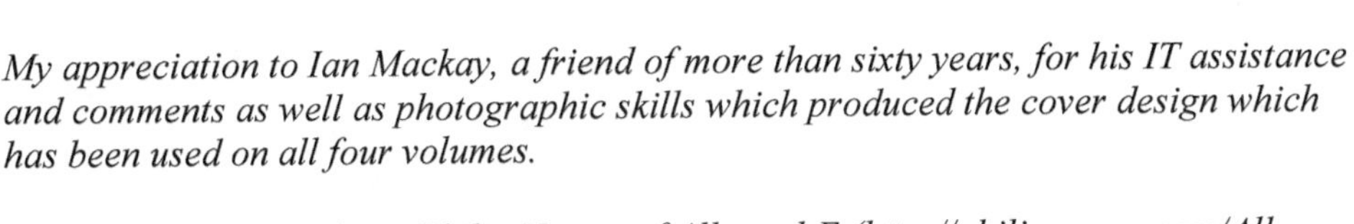
My appreciation to Ian Mackay, a friend of more than sixty years, for his IT assistance and comments as well as photographic skills which produced the cover design which has been used on all four volumes.

Thanks also to my editor, Philip Newey of All-read-E (http://philipnewey.com/All-read-E.htm) for editing the book and formatting the text.

Of course, any errors remain entirely my own. (The lawyers made me say this!)

PREFACE

"*No more writing*," he said to his wife as he finished writing the third book, Another 3,000 One Liners. "*I've got other things to do*."

I'll have to wait to see if this is true or just fake news, she thought nervously.

It turns out it was fake news. As new one liners emerged, the temptation to capture them and add others was too great to resist. Hence this fourth book, which brings the total of one liners in the combined four volumes to more than 17,000.

There comes a point in your life when you stop reading other people's books and write your own said Albert Einstein. So here goes again...

Humour is infectious. It lightens burdens, inspires hope, connects people, keeps us grounded, focused, alert, and happy. It is a universal language that stimulates both sides of the brain and allows us to get messages faster and remember them for longer.

Writing this book is a creative exploration in sharing thoughts that make me laugh, smile, and ponder. There are contributions from many hundreds of creative minds and, where possible, attributions have been made to acknowledge them.

Discovering and compiling these volumes was not an onerous task but rather a labour of love, with loads of enjoyment along the way. As Dorothy Parker so aptly put it, "Writing is the art of applying the arse to the seat."

There are many instances where, as you read, I know you'll nod your head in agreement as you recall these situations in your own experience.

Wisdom can also be found in short, sharp sentences. Wisdom has been defined as the reward you get for a lifetime of listening and reading when you'd have preferred to talk.

I hope that you, the reader, can open any page and get a chuckle, a laugh, a wry smile or a moment of reflection from one or more of the entries. "With mirth and laughter let old wrinkles come." (Shakespeare)

Humour is such a personal matter. Everybody can cry at the same material, but it's a lot harder to get everybody to laugh at the same thing.

This volume pays no deference to political correctness whatsoever, and there is the occasional entry that may be termed "adult humour", while religious items poke kindly fun at themselves.

Why this hard copy and not available as a digital book? The digital book cannot be infused with smells, won't flop open at favourite pages. Doesn't allow flowers to be pressed between its pages. Does not contain evidence of spilt tears or coffee stains. No, only a real book in print can do those things.

I have found that the real benefit of writing one liners is that you can leave out the parts that readers would have skipped anyway.

Please give me a sense of humour,
Give me the grace to see a joke,
To get some humour out of life,
And pass it on to other folk.

As a contribution to conservation this book was written using 100% recycled words.

Ray Prince

rprince@ozemail.com.au

About the author

Welcome to this, the fourth volume of Ray Prince's one liners, to add to his 4,000 One Liners, 5,000 One Liners, Another 3,000 One Liners which are available from the author.

This new volume presents a collection of new clever and enjoyable one liners carrying the same freshness that made the earlier volumes a success.

Ray won the Australian Speaking Championship of Toastmasters and then competed as one of the world finalists in the USA. He has also won the Toastmaster's Australian title for Humorous Speaking.

His career began with nine years practising his craft as an industrial chemist in the sugar manufacturing and oil refining industries and then subsequently graduating with a degree in economics, spending a further ten years as a consultant with the Queensland Division of the Australian Institute of Management.

Following this he spent twenty-two years as principal of his own management consulting business, working with major Australian companies.

During this period of his career, Ray was in demand as a national and international conference speaker in more than ten countries.

One of his interests has been collecting one liners for more than forty years.

He is retired and lives with his wife Margaret in Newport, south-east Queensland.

Ray's three earlier publications, have won acclaim:

"Over some fifty years I have known Ray and have a number of his books. His One Liner books are the funniest, most thought provoking and most entertaining.

"We recommend that you treat yourself to some of the hilarious examples in daily increments, if that is your way! Humour is excellent medicine."

Dr John Ryan
Medical Practitioner

“Like all of Ray's books, this one continues the tradition of a truly marvellous collection of one-liners. This volume brings the total of thoroughly entertaining sayings to more than 17,000 over the four volumes. It's a pity I can't use any of them in my job as a barrister but judges don't like smart alecs in court. I don't really understand why.

Read any of his other three One Liner volumes and you'll realise (if you don't know already) that life is absurdly amusing, and the law is about life. Most entries contain a germ of wisdom, but all of them are funny and clever.

"Buy them, and lighten up."

John Murphy
Barrister at Law

"As a long-haul frequent flyer, I often take one of Ray's four books with me to keep my mojo and sense of humour on the long trips. Always have a chuckle!

"It is very true that clever humour will make you laugh for seconds and think for minutes, and so much wisdom is available in so few words.

"I enjoy his collections so much I purchase copies of all of his One Liner books as gifts for friends and business associates!

"One liners are great ice breakers when meeting new clients."

Maurice Brand
Chairman & CEO
Global Energy Ventures Ltd

“As a management consultant I have been constantly addressing audiences, large and small, with both good news and "not so good news" about necessary changes at all business levels.

Having access to Ray's One Liner books, covering a wide range of subject matter with relevant real life amusing anecdotes, they never fail to supply to my messages the balance I seek for good understanding with a 'light' delivery. (The indexed categories are a time saver too!)

Of course I also quickly apply one of the thousands of Ray's one liners as a come-back when the Sergeant at Arms at our Rotary Meetings reveals one of my weaknesses, which also indicates the wide application available through this wonderfully entertaining "One Liners" resource”.

Boyd Fay
CEO
Management and Training Consultants

Copies of the four books of One Liners are available from the author at ***rprince@ozemail.com.au***

CONTENTS

FUN WITH ENGLISH

Dear John,

I want a man who knows what love is all about. You are generous, kind, thoughtful. People who are not like you admit to being useless and inferior. You have ruined me for other men. I yearn for you. I have no feelings whatsoever when we're apart. I can be forever happy. Will you let me be yours?

Jane.

Now see what a few commas, full stops, apostrophes etc. do when this letter which is punctuated in a completely different way.

Dear John,

I want a man who knows what love is. All about you are generous, kind, thoughtful people, who are not like you. Admit to being useless and inferior. You have ruined me. For other men, I yearn. For you, I have no feelings whatsoever. When we're apart, I can be forever happy. Will you let me be?

Yours,

Jane.

Any wonder people new to the English language have difficulty.

Some fun with words ...

This sentence can have seven different meanings depending on which word is stressed.

I did not say she stole my money. Try it.

Why, in pronouncing the word "Australia", is the letter "a" pronounced three different ways?

Word gymnastics: Laid is pronounced like paid but not said, and said is pronounced like bread but not bead, and bead is pronounced like lead not lead. Please explain.

English was not his first language, and he thought brussel sprouts was the name of a celebrity, so when he heard the expression "I hate brussel sprouts", he wondered what the poor bugger had done.

We say *in* January, *on* Wednesday and *at* 12 o'clock. Why?

What a waste. The word queue is just the letter q followed by four silent letters.

Yes, English can be weird. It can be understood through tough thorough thought though.

However, never make fun of anyone who speaks in broken English. It means they can speak another language. Can you?

Next time you try talking to a group of people who claim they can't speak English, just say, “OK, I'm about to punch everyone who's shoes are untied.”

You'll be amazed at how many people will look down.

FUN WITH ENGLISH

He was lost for words when his thesaurus was stolen.

People who say that I'm hard to shop for must not know where to buy books.

The problem with reading a good book is that you want to finish it but you don't want to finish it.

A house with a library in it has a soul. (Plato)

Don't ever sign anything until you pretend to read it first.

I'm reading a horror story in Braille. Something bad is about to happen ... I can feel it.

How come greenies want to save trees but love to read books?

Reading enables you to travel when you have to stay where you are.

Don't believe everything you read in public toilets. Sharon is not up for a good time. What an awkward phone call that was.

Young girl saw a picture in a zoo book and said, "Look at this! It's a frickin' elephant!" Actually it read "African elephant".

No need to read further; it gets worse from here.

If you are told you have got to stop watching so much TV and read more, just turn on the subtitles. Problem solved.

Google can bring you back 100,000 answers; a librarian can bring you back the right one without using Google.

Don't make jokes from mixed metaphors - too many other people have milked that bandwagon already.

Whoever is reading this quote is bored.

Tired apostrophes risk falling into a comma.

You know there is a problem with the education system when you realise that out of the 3 R’s only one begins with an "R".

There are two motives for reading a book: one, that you enjoy it; the other that you can boast about it.

After all the books I've read, I can't believe it took me this long to realise they are all written with just twenty-six letters rearranged in different order. What a rip-off.

I read part of it all the way through. (Samuel Goldwyn)

Parenthetical remarks (however relevant) are unnecessary.

Don't be redundant; don't use more words than necessary; it's highly superfluous.

If you want to read about love and marriage you'll have to buy two books.

In Australia, not reading poetry is the national pastime.

They say money cannot buy happiness, but I have a receipt from a bookstore telling a whole different story.

Reading teaches us how to be by ourself but never alone.

I cant believe there bringing back grammar school's.

Reading is dreaming with your eyes open.

If the English language made any sense, lackadaisical would have something to do with a shortage of flowers.

Reading is just staring at a dead piece of wood and hallucinating.

An appendix is that section of a book for which nobody has yet discovered any use.

With books you don't have to wait for the commercials to be over to find out what happens next.

Have you ever read a line so well written you just close the book and stare at the wall for a moment?

If a book is well written I always find it too short. (Jane Austen)

Unquestionably there is a word which contains all the vowels including "y".

You might call them swear words but I call them sentence enhancers.

Just made me some synonym rolls. Just like grammar used to make.

Nine tenths of existing books are nonsense, and the clever books are the refutation of that nonsense.

Never make fun of someone who mispronounces a word. It means they learned it by reading.

A book is what they make a movie out of for television.

Most new books are forgotten within a year, especially by those who borrow them.

It's could *have*, should *have*, would *have*, not *of ...* never *of.*

The ability to speak several languages is an asset, but your ability to keep your mouth shut in any language is priceless.

Life is like a grammar lesson. You find the past perfect and the present tense.

Cough, through, though, rough - none of these words rhyme, but for some godforsaken reason, goodonya and bologna do.

Bad grammar; don't go their.

A wise man once said nothing.

Is there a synonym for "synonym"? And I wonder if there's a euphemism for "euphemism".

I take it you already know of tough and bough and cough and dough.

Others may stumble but not you, on hiccough, thorough, tough and through.

A moth is not a moth in mother, nor both in bother, broth in brother.

If a woman is bad at parking it is only because she has been lied to regarding what fifteen centimetres is.

Because of COVID the National Spelling Bee competition has been ~~cancil~~.., ~~counsel~~.., ~~cansel~~.. Has been called off.

Help stamp out, eliminate and abolish redundancy.

I take for granite some people's poor grammar. More pacifically, for how there always thinking "for all intensive purposes" is supposably correct.

The first rule of the Thesaurus Club is that you don't talk about, mention, speak of, discuss, chin-wag, natter or chat about the Thesaurus Club.

Tense, moody, irregular? You must be a verb.

Every time I see someone write "tho" I think "ugh". (Which is exactly what is missing).

Three weeks without a signal typo!

She joined a book club. They primarily read wine labels.

Give me the shortest word in the English language that contains the letters: abcdef, i.e. give me your feedback.

Ever read some modern free verse and wonder who the hell set it free?

A classic book is one everyone is assumed to have read and often thinks they have.

A thesaurus is great. There's no other word for it.

Remember when text messaging was passing a note back and forth in class?

Second-hand bookshops are where I can find things I had no idea I wanted. (David Mitchell)

If you don't see the book on the shelf you want, write it.

With today's movies, if we took out all the bad language, we'd go back to silent films.

If people use the apostrophe incorrectly I'll be ill.

Don't ever date an apostrophe 'cos they are possessive.

After four centuries, the semicolon has finally achieved it's true calling: helping people wink online. ;-)

Reading Shakespeare is like wading through glue.

If you don't think punctuation is important, try forgetting the comma when you tell someone "I'm sorry, I love you".

The pregnant woman went into labour and started shouting, "Couldn't! Wouldn't! Shouldn't! Didn't! Can't!" - she was having contractions.

Avoid clichés like the plague. They're old hat.

People write congrats because they cannot spell congrajlashins.

People who do not use punctuation deserve a long sentence.

Do you ever have to battle between correcting grammar and having friends?

If you are going to insult, insult properly; it's "You're an idiot", not "Your an idiot".

Every time you make a typo the errorists win.

Frankly, I wonder who Frank was, and why he has an adverb all to himself.

That awkward moment when you spell something so wrong that autocorrect says, "I ain't got nothing, man."

An oxymoron walked into a bar and the silence was deafening.

Does anyone else have days when you wish you had a crappy education so other people's grammar wouldn't bother you so much?

Abstemious is a word which has the vowels in order and uncopyrightable is the longest word in the English language which does not have a repeating letter. Who knew?

ENGLISH EASY? NOT LIKELY!
(Foibles of Our Language)

PARADOXES often consist of ambiguity, mystery, absurdity, nonsense or humour, and hence add much to the enjoyment of humour in this book.

Enjoy these samples.

Discipline is just choosing between what you want now and what you want most.

The only way to have a friend is to be one. (Ralph Waldo Emerson)

Nobody can hurt me without my permission.

Paradoxically, minimalism is the maximum use of space.

You don't have to be interesting. You have to be interested.

Anyone can sympathise with the sufferings of a friend, but it requires a very fine nature to sympathise with a friend's success. (Oscar Wilde)

The shortest pencil is longer than the longest memory.

Be a man who was wise enough to bring into his service men who knew more than he. (Andrew Carnegie)

The reward of a thing done well is to have done it. (Ralph Waldo Emerson)

Don't handicap your children by making their lives easy.

Progress isn't made by early risers. It's made by lazy men trying to find easier ways to do something. (Robert Heinlein)

Butterflies are self-propelled flowers.

Belief gets in the way of learning.

Not knowing the answer to a question is not a valid excuse for making up a fairytale to explain it.

Some people insist that "mediocre" is better than "best". They delight in clipping wings because they themselves can't fly.

I came, I saw, she conquered. The original Latin seems to have been garbled.

When it's time to be counted, the important thing is to be man enough to stand up.

Don't try to explain computers to laymen. Simpler to explain sex to a virgin.

Never annoy an old dog; he might have one bite left.

Our life is what our thoughts make it. (Marcus Aurelius)

Everything is theoretically impossible, until it is done.

The measure of success is not whether you have a tough problem to deal with, but whether it's the same problem you had last year.

One of the sanest, surest, and most generous joys of life comes from being happy over the good fortune of others. (Robert Heinlein)

There is nothing so useless as doing efficiently that which should not be done.

The greatest mistake you can make in life is to be continually fearing you will make a mistake. (Elbert Hubbard)

What is left unsaid says it all.

If you say something is indescribable you are describing it. Similarly if you decide not to make a choice you have made a choice. Whoa!

Irony 

To check that irony is using language that normally signifies the opposite result typically for humorous or emphatic effect the following are offered. It can involve twists, wit and satire to cause a chuckle or at least a smile from you.

There could be no greater irony than dying in a living room.

For whatever reason, the pacifists are all up in arms about it - somewhat ironic?

Small doors at McDonald's.

Isn't it just a little ironic to see a group of pro-lifers throwing eggs at an abortion clinic?

Ten reasons why men are lazy: 1)

Religion: giving people hope in a world torn apart by religion.

Prince Charles has complained that modern people are far too materialistic. I wonder which of his palaces he was sitting in when he thought that one up?

Fat people having to resort to jogging pants when they can't get trousers to fit them.

Ten inches of snow during a global warming summit. Say again?

He has initiative but just needs to be told when to use it.

Irony is getting pregnant on a "pull-out" couch.

Procrastination day has been postponed.

I don't understand irony because I do not own an iron.

Sindeepa throws four unbiased coins and records the results. Calculate the probability we have used this name because we're scared of being called racist.

A sticker on the chicken packaging said "RSPCA Approved". Does everybody else see the irony of the RSPCA approving the slaughtering of birds?

In the last twelve months, Australia Post has received five million letters complaining about its service so, as a result, it's been able to announce record annual profits.

There's nothing more ironic than seeing a wet floor sign that has fallen over.

McDonald's are offering some great prizes, including a Mini Cooper which none of their customers will ever fit into.

My physics teacher says my understanding of forces is the worst he's ever known. Personally I think he's pushing my leg.

A company offered $50 for suggestions from staff that would save them money and awarded it to the employee who advised that they should only have $20 as the prize.

Anyone else find it ironic how professional boxers need security guards to walk them to the ring?

Being anaemic, irony isn't my strong point. (groan)

I haven't made a prediction in my life and I never will.

Oh the irony when somebody says, "I'm speechless."

Irony is having to make an appointment to see a clairvoyant.

There's got to be an online course that I can take to get over my internet addiction.

Fe, the ultimate irony. (Sorry, but the author is a chemist)

The emblem for the New Zealand Air force is the flightless kiwi!

It's not fair - the further forward you move the car seat because you're short, the taller you have to be to reach the seatbelt.

A man called me pretentious the other day. If you ask me, that's like the basin calling the cauldron ebony.

Studies have shown that 1 in every 49.5 people is an amputee.

They say sarcasm is the lowest form of wit, as if I've never heard that before.

I think my efforts to cut down on using clichés are going well. I'm just taking each day as it comes and giving it 110%.

For the whole of their childhood, we tell children not to go out after dark, not to talk to strangers, and not to take sweets from anyone they don't know. Then every year there is Halloween.

Skinny jeans - XXL. WTF?

Ironically, I seem to forget Remembrance Day every year.

There's something beautifully ironic about an email confirming that I've successfully unsubscribed from an email list.

Being anti-protest, he had no way of showing it.

Surely the phrase "drinking problem" is an oxymoron?

It's a bugger if thieves steal your burglar alarm.

An enormously fat, perfectly round woman named Dot. How ironical.

The Hairdressers Union are against cuts.

Isn't it ironic that most jokes that start with "Isn't it ironic ..." aren't ironic?

The word plagiarism originally derives from another word.

Love oxymorons. Despise contradictory statements.

Irony: looking for a *Where's Wally* book.

Have you noticed you can only take diet pill's on a full stomach?

Being badly beaten with a first-aid kit is surely ironic.

Statistically, 3.14 out of 10 obese mathematicians will get this.

My girlfriend just called me ignorant. I have absolutely no idea what she's talking about.

Ironically, when you wear camouflage, it makes you stand out more.

Why is it so hard to remember how to spell "mnemonic"?

Have you ever hit your elbow and found it even slightly funny?

Phobophobia - fear of having a phobia.

She always worries when she goes to bed that she's going to wake up dead.

Her smoke alarm blew up and burnt her house down.

I found a website today for anorexics; it boasts about being the largest one.

I immediately hate people who make snap judgements.

Does anyone else find it ironic that you need a pair of scissors to get into a new pair of scissors pack?

You don't understand the superiority theory like I do.

It's a bit ironic that the breast implant clinic has gone bust.

Aphorisms

While aphorisms are short clever sayings that are intended to express a general truth, here you can find many truths that you already know.

Parents are the last people on earth who ought to have children.

The golden rule is that there are no golden rules. (George Bernard Shaw)

How come families with children and families without children are sorry for each other.

The only problem with having nothing to do is you can't stop and rest.

You live only once, but if you do it right, once is enough. (Mae West)

If everything seems to be going well, you have obviously overlooked something.

Vulgarity is simply the conduct of other people. (Oscar Wilde)

Conscience is a mother-in-law whose visit never ends.

Hospital is a place where they wake you up to give you a sleeping pill.

It is a waste of energy to be angry with a man who behaves badly, just as it is to be angry with a car that won't go. (Bertrand Russel)

Everybody wants to save the earth; nobody wants to help their mother do the dishes.

Your children need your presence more than your presents.

He tested the aphorism, "A watched pot never boils." Boiled the same amount of water in the same kettle sixty-two times. In some cases he ignored the kettle; in others, he watched it intently. In every instance, the water reaches its boiling point in precisely 51.7 seconds. So what's with this aphorism?

You can't always get what you want, but if you try, sometimes you get what you need. (The Rolling Stones)

Pure and simple? The truth never is.

For every minute you are angry you lose a minute of happiness.

Do, or do not; there is no try. (Yoda, *Star Wars*)

Failure is not falling down, it is the refusal to get back up.

Political Correctness

Political correctness is opinion, not fact, and who do these PC-pushing people think they are to even suggest that their opinion might be of more value than mine? (Ray Prince)

I am responsible for what I say but I am not responsible for what you think or understand.

Just because you are offended doesn't mean you are right.

The worst form of equality is to try to make unequal things equal. (Aristotle)

The world is a magical place full of people waiting to be offended by something.

Throw me to the wolves and I shall return leading the pack.

Hey, you social engineers. Happiness is letting every situation be what it is instead of what you think it should be.

Instead of raising your voice improve your argument.

If people say your morals are old fashioned just point out that you were brought up properly.

Caution: the media does not reflect reality.

Why be politically correct when you can be right.

Politically correct people get offended because someone somewhere might be offended.

Wishing you a what-ever-doesn't-offend-you day.

I do not agree with what you say but I will defend to the death your right to say it.

Political correctness is one of the main engines of nannyism.

If you lose one sense, others become enhanced. That is why when people lose their sense of humour they have a heightened sense of self-importance.

Political correctness does not change people; it just shuts them up.

If only PC stood for political courage rather than political correctness.

Well, daughter dear, political correctness is when you surrender your opinions and freedom of speech to appease a pack of whining whinging sooks and pansies who need everything sugar-coated for them.

Breaking news: your sexuality is not unique and nobody cares.

Anyone feel offended because you no longer can offend anyone?

"Poor people are poor because of rich people" is the same as "slow cars are slow because of fast cars".

The greatest enemy of clear language is insincerity. (George Orwell)

My wife complained that I'm too old fashioned. "Nonsense", I said. "Now get thee gone, wench, back to the scullery from wherest thou came and cease thoust chatter o'er much ado about nothing, brazen harlot."

It's called a joke. We used to tell them before people became offended by everything.

Just legalise everything and let Darwin do the rest.

My parents spanked me as a child. As a result I now suffer from a psychological condition called "respect for others".

The further a society drifts from the truth the more it will hate people who speak it.

Anyone yearn for the days when jokes did not have to be politically correct and were funny too?

AGELESS FROLICS

The writer is aged eighty-one at the time of writing this book, which explains the flavour of many of the following. Even though you might be at the tender age of fifty (or even less), with some luck and a sense of fun and laughter you'll reach this milestone as well.

A man asks his doctor, "Do you think I'll live to be a hundred?"

The doctor asks the man, "Well, that depends. Do you drink?"

"Oh, no sir! I abstain from all alcohol. Soft drink, too. I just drink plenty of fresh water."

"Do you smoke?"

"No, sir! Never smoked in my life, and I stay away from any place with second-hand smoke."

"Do you eat a lot of sugary and greasy foods?"

"No, sir! I carefully watch my diet and caloric intake, and I'm sure to eat plenty of vegetables."

"Do you go to parties? Stay up late? Are you sexually promiscuous?"

"Not at all! Early to bed and early to rise! And abstinence is key."

The doctor raises an eyebrow at the man. "So, why exactly do you want to live to be a hundred?"

An older lady walks into a cocktail bar and the bartender asks for ID. "You've got to be kidding," she said. "I'm almost sixty years old."

The bartender apologised, but said he had to see the licence. The lady showed her ID, then paid and told the bartender to keep the change. "The tip's for asking me for ID," she said.

The bartender put the change in the tip cup. "Thanks," he said. "Works every time."

Anyone remember when you played "King of the Hill" on piles of gravel left on vacant construction sites and, when you got hurt, Mum pulled out the forty-eight cent bottle of mercurochrome (kids liked it better because it didn't sting like iodine did) and then you got your arse spanked?

Now it's a trip to the emergency room, followed by a ten-day dose of a $49 bottle of antibiotics, and then Mum calls the lawyer to sue the contractor for leaving a horribly vicious pile of gravel where it was such a threat.

To top it off, not a single person had ever been told that they were from a dysfunctional family.

This is something that happened at an assisted living centre.

The people who live there have small apartments but they all eat at a central cafeteria. One morning one of the residents didn't show up for breakfast, so my wife went upstairs to see if everything was OK.

She could hear him through the door and he said that he was running late and would be down shortly, so she went back to the dining area.

An hour later he still hadn't arrived so she went back up and she found him on the stairs. He was coming down the stairs but was having a hell of time. He had a death grip on the hand rail and seemed to have trouble getting his legs to work right.

She told him she was going to call an ambulance but he told her no, he wasn't in any pain and just wanted to have his breakfast. So she helped him the rest of the way down and he had his breakfast.

When he tried to return to his room he was completely unable to get up even the first step so they called an ambulance for him.

A couple of hours later she called the hospital to see how he was doing. The receptionist there said he was fine; he just had both of his legs in one leg of his boxer shorts.

Send this to your children so that they don't sell your house before they know the facts.

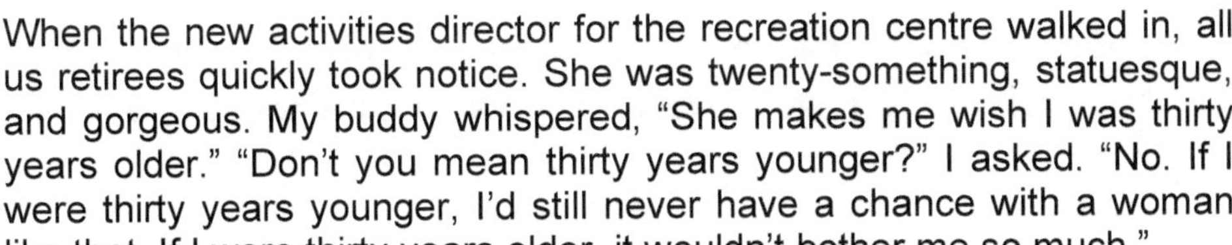

When the new activities director for the recreation centre walked in, all us retirees quickly took notice. She was twenty-something, statuesque, and gorgeous. My buddy whispered, “She makes me wish I was thirty years older.” “Don’t you mean thirty years younger?” I asked. “No. If I were thirty years younger, I’d still never have a chance with a woman like that. If I were thirty years older, it wouldn’t bother me so much.”

AGELESS FROLICS

On Getting Older

Your kids are becoming you ... but your grandchildren are perfect.

You forget names ... but it's OK, because other people forget they even know you.

You realise you're never going to be really good at anything ... especially golf.

You sleep better on a lounge chair with the TV blaring than in bed. It's called "pre-sleep".

You miss the days when everything worked with just an "ON" and "OFF" switch.

You tend to use more four letter words ... "what?" ... "when?"

Now that you can afford expensive jewellery, it's not safe to wear it anywhere.

What used to be freckles are now liver spots.

Everybody whispers.

When I was a kid I wanted to be older, but this is not what I expected.

It's probably my age that tricks people into thinking I'm an adult.

Does anyone else think growing older would take longer?

Never sing in the shower! Singing leads to dancing, dancing leads to slipping, and slipping leads to paramedics seeing you naked. So remember, don't sing!

I'm at a place in my life where errands are starting to count as going out.

If you can't think of a word say, "I forgot the English word for it." That way people will think you're bilingual instead of an idiot.

At least you're not as old as you will be next year.

After forty, a body has a mind of its own.

OK, so you're not as young as you used to be, but you're not as old as you're going to be.

Being over seventy I learn something new every day ... and forget five other things.

Two important lessons in life: can't recall the first, but the second is to write everything down.

You're getting old when you get the same sensation from a rocking chair that you once got from a roller coaster.

Don't be worried about your smartphone or TV spying on you. Your vacuum cleaner has been collecting dirt on you for years.

At what point can we just start using 2020 as profanity? As in: "That's a load of 2020"; or "What in the 2020?"; or "abso-2020-lutely".

I've reached an age when my train of thought often leaves the station without me.

The older I get, the older old is.

Old age is no places for sissies. (Bette Davis)

You're getting old when you get that one candle on the cake and they say, "See if you can blow this out."

Try to avoid things that make you fat, like scales, mirrors and photos.

No matter how old I get, I will always be overly excited when I receive a handwritten letter in the mail.

Bean bag chairs are Venus fly traps for anyone over fifty.

Current fashion style is "clothes that still fit".

No matter how old you are, an empty Christmas wrapping paper tube is still a light sabre.

Men, you know you are going bald when it takes you longer each morning to wash your face.

She put her scales in the bathroom corner and said they will stay there until they apologise.

The great thing about getting old is that pissing people off is both expected and enjoyable.

You reach an age when you can remember going through a whole day without taking a picture of anything.

Life is short. Smile while you still have teeth.

You are getting old when you decide to procrastinate.

You're not old in comparison to the age of the earth.

Do you now go to bed at the time you used to go out?

Getting old is when everything dries up or leaks.

While you can only be young once, you can always be immature.

The older I get, the earlier it gets late and the more dangerous it is to sneeze.

You know you are getting middle aged when you have a party and the neighbours don't even realise it.

You are middle aged when you quit trying to hold your stomach in, no matter who walks into the room.

It's been a rough week, but I don't need bail money so it could have been worse.

It is easier to get older than it is to get wiser.

Ever forgotten what you have forgotten?

Ever find your knees buckle but your belt won't?

The good old days were when we weren't good and we weren't old.

If you're still awake at 2 am it's indigestion only if you are middle aged.

Middle age is when you choose your cereal for the fibre, not the toy.

Middle age is that period in a man's life when he'd rather not have a good time than have to get over it. (Oscar Wilde)

You're only young once. After that you have to think up some other excuse.

Adolescence is a period of rapid changes. Between the ages of twelve and seventeen, for example, a parent ages as much as twenty years.

Getting older is pretty much just paying bills and finally understanding why killers in horror movies target teenagers.

I'm at the delusional age when everybody looks far older than I do.

At my age, if I see that a coin lying on the ground is anything less than a fifty-cent piece it isn't worth the aches and pains of leaning over to pick it up.

It's a bugger that age is such a high price to pay for maturity.

As men get older toys become more expensive.

I will never be old. To me old age is fifteen years older than I am.

Anyone can get old. All you have to do is live long enough.

I have a profound respect for age, especially if it is bottled.

And just like that, 1970 was fifty+ years ago.

I am "My first car had an ashtray" years old.

At what age will I grow out of not answering the door when I'm home alone and sneaking around the house to see who is knocking?

Someone left a list in the supermarket cart that said, "Cheese and shit." My soulmate is out there somewhere.

Some call it multi-tasking, but I call it doing something else while I try to remember what I was doing in the first place.

If you haven't grown up by the age of fifty you don't have to.

The age of a woman doesn't mean a thing. The best tunes are played on the oldest fiddles.

When you drop something when you are younger you pick it up. When you are older, you stare at it for a bit, contemplating whether you actually need it anymore.

I'm now at the age when I've got to prove that I'm just as good as I never was. (Rex Harrison)

If you see me smiling it's because I'm thinking of doing something evil or naughty. If you see me laughing it's because I've already done it.

Her nickname was smoke detector since she was both loud and annoying.

The year you start lying about your age has finally arrived.

Getting old is when people call at 9.00 pm and ask if they woke you.

I'm now at the age when jeans are considered formal wear.

The best part about getting older is … nothing! Getting older sucks.

Old enough to know better, but young enough to do it anyway.

He who buys what he does not need steals from himself. (Swedish proverb)

The older one gets the more one's body pops more than bubble wrap.

Old age is when you wink at a girl and she says, “Is there something wrong with your eyes?”

When you retire, you switch bosses - from the one who hired you to the one who married you.

When you retire and time is no longer a matter of urgent importance, your colleagues generally present you with a watch.

You have to put off being young until you can retire.

For most people, growing up in the sixties was a lot more fun than being in their sixties.

It is better to live rich than to die rich. (Samuel Johnson)

Retire from work, but not from life.

It's hard to be nostalgic when you can't remember anything.

The difference between astronomy and astrology is approximately sixty IQ points.

Life insurance is a contract that keeps you poor all your life so you can die rich.

Career hint: there is no future in writing history books.

Dense people are like glow sticks where you have to shake the crap out of them until the light comes on.

Retirement is doing nothing and not worrying about being caught at it.

Adolescence is when a boy has reached the age when he knows why a strapless gown must be held up, but doesn't understand how.

He was so old he must have been around when Long John Silver had two legs and an egg on his shoulder.

Just when you think you are home and dry, the checkout girl finds an item without a price on it.

Things in my life are finally starting to click, like my elbows, my knees, etc.

The years that a woman subtracts from her age are not lost; they are added to the ages of other women.

Senescence begins and middle age ends the day your descendants outnumber your friends. (Ogden Nash)

The distinctive facial features of a parent are poor people's paternity test. Rich people use DNA.

You know you are getting old when you have to scroll down, and scroll down some more, to select the year you were born when completing on-line forms.

Remember the good old days, when no one had a clue what "gluten" was?

Why is it old people say "There's no place like home", yet when you put them in one ...?

By the time a man is wise enough to watch his step, he's too old to go anywhere.

Is there a refund for this thing called being an adult?

The modern teenager won't listen to advice from an old person, defined as a person who remembers when there was no Velcro.

Old is when you buy a sexy sheer nightgown and don't know anyone who can see through it.

By the time we find greener pastures, we're too old to climb the fence.

Aging gracefully is like the nice way of saying you're slowly looking worse.

If you taught your children, you won't have to raise your grandchildren.

Remember the good old days when kids were scared to death of their parents?

We grow too soon old and too late smart. (Dutch proverb)

Retired. Under New Management. (See spouse for details)

You're never too old to become younger.

Each year over sixty, one more part of your body becomes audible.

At my age, I stopped buying green bananas.

At my age, at midnight I'm surprised to find it is only 8 pm.

When I was young I wanted to be older. This crap is not what I expected.

When we were young the streets were our PlayStation.

Pee into a toilet and it never fills up. Explain that, scientists!

I never use my car indicators because it's nobody's business where I'm going.

Wrinkles don't hurt.

The only things that old age comes standard with are grey hair and wrinkles. Wisdom and intellect are earned.

There might be grey on the roof but there is still fire in the oven.

Can you remember when multiplication was called "times table"?

RELIGIOUS PLAYFULNESS
(For the Priestly and Others)

Here is a short version of ten commandments for you time-pressed folks or, as you prefer to be known, lazy.

1. God rules.
2. Images are copyrighted.
3. Swear in moderation.
4. Sunday double time.
5. Honour stuff.
6. Only kill what you eat or dislike.
7. Cheat not, unless pushed.
8. Steal considerately.
9. Don't lie much.
10. Ass. Don't go there.

This simple list of rules is regularly and repeatedly broken by politicians, bankers, media commentators, celebrities and religious leaders.

Sean is the vicar of a protestant parish and Patrick is the priest at the Roman Catholic Church across the road.

One day they are seen together, erecting a sign which says:

"THE END IS NEAR. TURN YOURSELF AROUND NOW BEFORE IT IS TOO LATE."

As a car speeds past them, the driver leans out his window and yells, "Leave people alone, you religious nutters. We don't need your lectures."

From around the next curve they hear screeching tyres and a big splash.

Shaking his head, Father Patrick says, "Dat's da terd one dis mornin'."

“Yaa," Sean agrees, then adds, "Do ya tink maybe da sign should just say 'BRIDGE CLOSED'?"

An atheist goes to a humble country church and, after exchanging cordial greetings, the atheist notices a beautiful silver and gold model of the earth and solar system on the minister's desk.

"That's amazing," the atheist said. "I'd love one of those. Who made it?"

"Oh, nobody made it. It just happened."

Three blokes are fishing when an angel appears.

The first guy says, “I’ve suffered from back pain for years. Can you help me?” The angel touches the man’s back, and he feels instant relief.

The second guy points to his thick glasses and begs for a cure for his poor eyesight. When the angel tosses the lenses into the lake, the man regains 20/20 vision.

As the angel turns to the third fellow, he instantly recoils and screams, “Don’t touch me! I’m on disability welfare!”

A rabbi said to a precocious six-year-old boy, "So your mother says your prayers for you each night? That's very commendable. What does she say?"

The little boy replied, "Thank God he's in bed!"

A distraught man runs up and down a train looking for a Catholic priest. "Is there a priest on board? I need a priest."

A gentle parson says, "Can I help, sir? I am a Lutheran/ Baptist/ Methodist/Anglican minister [choose your religion to insert]. Can I help you in any way?"

The man replies, "Probably not, because I am looking for a bottle opener."

RELIGIOUS PLAYFULNESS

Honk your horn if you love Jesus. Text while driving if you'd like to meet him.

Live your life so people won't have to lie at your funeral.

The Lord is not my shepherd for I am not a sheep.

He's going to hell in so many different religions.

Anyone who believes that men are the equal of women has never seen a man trying to wrap a Christmas present.

Bacon proves that God has a sense of humour. He invents the greatest meat in the world then doesn't let his chosen people eat it.

To be a prosperous pastor one needs: (1) a Bible (2) a tailored suit; and (3) a few psychology books. (Mokokoma Mokhonoana)

To some, faith is just intellectual laziness.

Confessions may be great for your soul, but they are hell for your reputation.

The wages of sin are death, but the working conditions are great.

Even before Christmas has said "Hello", it's saying "Buy Buy".

On my way to church and when almost there, I looked at my mobile and it said, "No service," so I turned around and went home.

Christmas is a baby shower that went totally overboard.

You can tell a lot about a person by the way they handle three things: a rainy day, lost luggage, and tangled Christmas tree lights.

The office Christmas party is a great opportunity to catch up with people you haven't seen for twenty minutes.

If you've seen one Santa, you've seen a mall.

Aren't we forgetting the true meaning of Christmas. You know, the birth of Santa?

Oh for the good old days when people would stop Christmas shopping when they ran out of money.

When I stand before God at the end of my life, I would hope that I would not have a single bit of talent left, and could say, "I used everything you gave me." (Erma Bombeck)

If you can't wrap Christmas presents well, at least make it look like they put up a good fight.

The trouble with being a god is that you've got no one to pray to.

God give me patience, because if you give me strength I'll finish up in prison.

Ever walked into a mosque and thought you were in the middle a yoga session?

You should be worried. God knows all about you.

All the animals are on board and accounted for, Noah, but I've got bad news. The unicorns are gay.

What did they feed the lions and tigers with in the ark, sir?

Men never do evil so completely and cheerfully as when they do it from a religious conviction. (Blaise Pascal)

Our economy is so bad, Lent next year will be called borrowed.

Sin lies only in hurting others unnecessarily. All other "sins" are invented nonsense. Hurting yourself is not sinful - just stupid. (Robert Heinlein)

When God sneezed, I didn't know what to say.

"Jesus loves you" is a great thing to hear in church but horrible to hear in a Mexican prison.

Goodness is about what you do, not who you pray to.

Some people talk about finding God, as if He or She could get lost.

Gods don't like people not doing much work. People who aren't busy all the time might start to think. (Terry Pratchett)

If we're all equal in the sight of God, how come the head of a convent is called Mother Superior?

Why would God put the appendix in you when it does nothing but randomly kill you for no reason?

My favourite part of the Bible is the part where that old guy says, "We're going to need a bigger boat."

Churches aren't half empty, they're just too big.

If maths was taught like creationism, then 2+2=5 would be a "competing theory".

What does it mean when holy water sizzles when it touches your skin? (Just asking for a friend.)

His ego was such that he looked like he was waiting for a vacancy in the Trinity.

You can't take it with you. Evidence? Ever seen a hearse with a tow bar?

You can't teach an old dogma new tricks. (Dorothy Parker)

The capacity for friendship is God's way of apologising for our families.

If heaven really exists, then heaven is the job, hell is unemployment, while life is merely an interview.

No sinner is ever saved after the first twenty minutes of a sermon.

Even the longest book that is read was written one word at a time.

After that whale ate him, I bet Jonah cancelled his subscription to Greenpeace.

The Popemobile: because nothing says, "I have faith in God!" like four inches of bulletproof glass.

Keep this in mind. A clergyman is simply a ticket speculator outside the gates of Heaven.

boy, boy, boy, boy, boy, boy, BOY, boy, boy, boy, boy, boy, boy, is the seating arrangement at the Last Supper.

Be an optimist at least until they start moving animals in pairs to Cape Kennedy.

Wearing things such as makeup and fake hair is some people's subconscious way of showing God where He made a mistake.

A belief is just an uneducated guess. (Mokokoma Mokhonoana)

The devil whispered to me, "I'm coming for you." I whispered back, "Bring a pizza."

Moses wandered lost in the wilderness for forty years because, even in biblical times, men would not stop to ask for directions.

The number of people who believe in religious teachings far outweighs that of those who practise them.

I can't be the only one frightened when our mega-sized houses of worship sound like they could take on Godzilla.

If we are all God's children, what's so special about Jesus?

If Jesus was a Jew, how come he has a Mexican first name? (Billy Connolly)

I wrapped my Christmas presents early this year but accidentally used Happy Birthday paper. I didn't want to waste it so I just wrote "Jesus" on it. Problem solved.

While it's a miracle Jesus was able to turn water into wine, I thank God each morning for giving me the ability to turn water into coffee.

Religion is like a pair of shoes ... find one that fits you but don't make me wear your shoes.

Religion is a culture of faith; science is a culture of doubt. (Richard P Feynman)

Adam and Eve had many advantages, but the principal one was that they escaped teething.

When the Pope dies is he being promoted or fired?

Dear Pope, religion and birth control are more compatible than you may think. Every time a condom breaks, someone learns to pray.

There is no difference between someone who eats too little and sees Heaven and someone who drinks too much and sees snakes. (Bertrand Russell)

When you lose a follower on Twitter you know how Jesus feels every day.

Merry Christmas everyone, and Happy Birthday Jesus without a Facebook reminder.

Jesus loves you, but I'm his favourite.

We are all atheists about most of the gods that societies have ever believed in. Some of us just go one god further. (Richard Dawkins)

The trouble with half-truths is that people tend to believe the wrong half.

Church is like gym to some people. No matter what they do all week, they think they can erase it with one visit.

If Eve cursed the entire human race just for an apple, I can only imagine what she would have done for a Snickers.

The road to Hell is paved with everything that feels like Heaven.

A Christian is one who believes that the New Testament is a divinely inspired book admirably suited to the spiritual needs of his neighbour, or one who follows the teachings of Christ in so far as they are not inconsistent with a life of sin. (Ambrose Bierce)

When religious people complain, you think, "What, praying didn't work?"

If God can't prove he exists, what makes you think you can?

Science doesn't care what you believe.

How to become an atheist. 1. Choose any god other than your own. 2. Analyse why you do not believe in it. 3. Now apply the same logic to your own.

The crime of blasphemy was invented by priests for the purpose of defending doctrines not able to take care of themselves. (RG Ingersoll)

And the Lord said unto John, "Come forth and receive eternal life." But John came fifth and won a toaster.

Religion is like a buffet. People take what they like and ignore the rest.

My favourite part of the Bible is when Jesus is talking to God (himself) and someone who wasn't there is writing about it.

He maintains he is a creationist because man created God.

If money is the root of all evil, why do they ask for it in church?

The biggest miracle Jesus performed was being a white guy in the Middle East, and how the hell did he find people named Peter, John, James, Matthew, Andrew, Philip, Thomas and Simon in the Middle East?

I know God doesn't make mistakes, but I question some of the places he put hair on the human body.

Basically, religion is, "If it feels good - stop."

Jack and Jill went up the hill to fetch a pail of water. But with your help, we can put a well in their home village. (Christian Missionary Outreach)

Going to war over religion is basically just killing people in an argument over who has the better imaginary friend.

If you are tired of all my anti-religious jokes why don't you pray for me to stop?

And the Three Wise Men said to Jesus, "Just to be clear, these gifts are for your birthday *and* Christmas."

God talks to you? There's medication for that.

Say what you like about the ten commandments, you must always come back to the pleasant fact that there are only ten of them.

The devil came in all his glory to tempt and recruit me, realised who he was talking to, apologised, and asked me for a job application instead.

When one person sees an invisible man they are a nut case; one hundred people see him it's a cult; ten million people see him it's a respected religion.

The religious diet is where you eat anything you like then pray for a miracle.

If a Jehovah's Witness dies and goes to heaven does God hide behind the Pearly Gates and pretend he's not home?

An apology for the devil: it must be remembered that we have heard only one side of the case; God has written all the books. (Samuel Butler)

Please, God, help me lose weight but keep my boobs.

If God had really intended man to fly, He'd make it easier to get to the airport.

If God didn't think humility was important, he would have put the prostate somewhere else.

There are 473 tiles on my church's ceiling.

The missionaries go forth to Christianise the savages - as if the savages weren't dangerous enough already.

Christianity has a whole religion based on a woman who really stuck to her story.

Religion is what stops the poor from murdering the rich. (Napoleon Bonaparte)

If you've ever watched a butcher wrap pork chops, you've seen me wrapping Christmas presents.

I'm dreaming of a white Christmas, but if the white runs out I'll drink the red.

If you got a big-screen TV for Christmas, be sure to put the empty box out with your neighbour's trash. That way, their house will get robbed instead of yours.

Don't send funny greeting cards for birthdays or Christmas. Save them for funerals when their cheery effect is really needed. (PJ O'Rourke)

The Opposition's supporters are like Christmas lights. Half don't work and the other half are not very bright.

By the way, Santa has seen your Facebook entries and is giving you a dictionary next Christmas.

An easy way to tell people you don't like them is to send them a Christmas card with loads of loose glitter in it.

I do not feel obliged that the same God who endowed us with sense, reason, and intellect has intended us to forgo their use. (Galileo Galilei)

Why is it that after you've mailed your last Christmas card, you will receive a card from someone you overlooked?

Want to make a fortune? Open a business that untangles Christmas lights.

Thanks once again to autocorrect, my sister's kids are expecting the Easter Rabbi tomorrow.

Lent was invented so Christians could take another shot at their New Year's resolutions.

God is good, but never dance in a small boat. (Proverb)

In the beginning there was nothing, which exploded.

Gods like to see an atheist around - gives them something to aim at.

Does anyone know what page of the Bible explains how to turn water into wine? Asking for a friend.

As I dropped my phone in the toilet are all my phone friends baptised?

No amount of belief makes something a fact.

Religions are basically guilt with different holidays.

As you walk through the valley of the shadow of death remind yourself that you can't always trust Google Maps.

In final exams half the students are praying to God while the other half are trying to make deals with Satan.

BROAD BRIEF BUSINESS BITS
(MAINLY MONEY MATTERS)

A set of company accounts:

Advertise for typist	$ 150
Flowers for typist's desk	$ 25
Week's salary for typist	$ 620
Roses for typist	$ 55
Chocolates for wife	$ 22
Lunch - typist & self	$ 95
Typist's salary	$ 740
Movies - wife & self	$ 61
Theatre - typist & self	$ 340
Chocolates for wife	$ 32
Lillian's salary	$ 880
Theatre, dinner - Lillian & self	$ 565
Medical treatment – Lillian	$ 950
Fur for wife	$7800
Advertisement, male typist	$ 160

In heaven, Einstein is being introduced to his room mates.

"See, here is your first room mate. He has an IQ of 180!"

"Why that's wonderful!" says Albert. *"We can discuss mathematics!"*

"And here is your second room mate. His IQ is 150!"

"Why that's wonderful!" says Albert. *"We can discuss quantum physics!"*

"And here is your third room mate. His IQ is 100!"

"That's wonderful! We can discuss the latest plays at the theatre!"

Just then another man moves out to capture Albert's hand and shake it.

"I'm your last room mate and I'm sorry, but my IQ is only 80."

Albert smiles and says, *"So, where do you think interest rates are headed?"*

I went to my local market today and saw a sign that said: "ONE WATERMELON FOR $3 OR THREE FOR $10"

Instead of telling the guy behind the stall how stupid the sign was I decided to show him.

So I walked up to him and asked, "Can I buy a watermelon please?"

"Yes, sir, that'll be three dollars."

I handed over the money and asked, "Actually, can I have another one please?"

"No problem, sir, that's three dollars."

"Can I have one more?"

"Certainly, sir, three dollars."

Smirking I said, "I've just bought three watermelons for nine dollars but on your sign it says ten. Don't you realise how stupid you are?"

"That happens a lot," he smiled, "until I point out that you just bought three watermelons instead of one."

Moral: Don't mess with farmers.

He shows up late for work.

The boss yells, "You should have been here at 8.30!"

He replies, "Why? What happened?"

Driving back from Bundaberg, I stopped at a vegetable stand. It was deserted except for a sleeping German shepherd. I stepped over the dog, helped myself to some corn cobs, then opened the honour cashbox to pay. Taped to the inside of the lid was this note: "The dog can count."

There is a theory that at Christmas time there is a cohort of street kids who wait until Santa has gone down the chimney then they rip off stuff from his sleigh and sell it at the next weekend's markets.

Went to my bank to deposit a cheque, and they asked me for ID. I said, "Are you telling me other people are trying to put money into my account and you're telling them no?"

BROAD BRIEF BUSINESS BITS (MAINLY MONEY MATTERS)

All I've ever wanted was an honest week's pay for an honest day's work.

Customers are people who indirectly pay for all your vacations, hobbies, and golf games and give you the opportunity to better yourself.

Wonder how my bankruptcy accountant thinks I'm going to pay him.

Work spares us from three great evils: boredom, vice and need. (Voltaire)

Motivation: Going to work for a large organisation is like getting on a train. Are you going sixty miles an hour or is the train going sixty miles an hour and you're just sitting still?

Work is the greatest thing, so we should always save some of it for tomorrow.

There are no office hours for leaders.

Anyone who has not done one half their day's work by ten o clock, runs a chance of leaving the other half undone.

Work eight hours and sleep eight hours but not the same hours.

A deficit is what you have when you don't have as much as if you had nothing.

In a finance firm avoid pretentious job titles like Lord of the Realm, Defender of the Faith, Emperor of Siberia or Audit partner.

Early to bed, early to rise, work like hell and advertise.

The problem with paradigms is that shift happens.

If you're not making money or you're not having fun, what the hell are you doing in business?

If women are expected to do the same work as men, we must teach them the same things. (Plato)

Don't be upset with the results you didn't get from the work you didn't do.

Work hard and save your money and when you are old you will be able to buy the things only the young can enjoy.

If you tell the boss you were late for work because you had a flat tire, the next morning you will have a flat tire

Does the wage gap mean women get to leave work 23% early today?

A committee can make a decision that is dumber than any of its members.

This law firm, as you know, prohibits sex between us and our clients to prevent clients being billed twice for the same service.

Don't give up running your business. Remember Moses was once a basket case.

A nillionaire is a person with little or no money.

If someone is laughing then laugh with them. If they are singing then sing with them. If they are working, let them work ... you do not want to ruin their concentration.

Perseverance is the hard work you do after you get tired of doing the hard work you already did.

Every organisation is perfectly designed to get the results they are getting.

Pretty soon, we are going to be e-mailing Nigerians about depositing money electronically.

The simplest way to explain the behaviour of any bureaucratic organisation is to assume that it is controlled by a group of its enemies.

Gold Lotto is many people putting in a lot of their money to make someone a millionaire.

The way taxes are you may as well marry for love.

If love is more important than money, try paying your bills with a hug.

Stuck between "You need to save money" and "You only live once".

LinkedIn is just a dating site for people with a job.

Not many people know that Wizard of Light Bulb Moments is the title of a Marketing Director.

Intellectuals solve problems; geniuses prevent them. (Albert Einstein)

The difference between tax avoidance and tax evasion is about ten years.

Gold Lotto is just a tax on hope.

You are stuck with your debt if you can't budge it.

Over the past three decades there has been a history of replacing what worked with what sounded good. (Thomas Sowell)

Why is the death of a billionaire worth more to the media than the lives of a billion poor people?

Business conventions are important because they demonstrate how many people a company can operate without.

Camping is nature's way of promoting the motel business. (Dave Barry)

Business people talk golf all morning at the office, and business all afternoon on the links.

Business is something which, if you don't have any, you go out of.

Smooth seas do not make skilful sailors. (African proverb)

I think my postman is stealing my Nigerian lottery cheques.

Never put decisions in the hands of people who pay no price for being wrong.

Just when I saw the light at the end of the tunnel, it turned out to be some bastard bringing me the latest tax updates.

Always dream of being a millionaire like my uncle. He's dreaming too.

No nation has ever taxed itself into prosperity.

A committee is the only known form of life with dozens of bellies and no brain.

Clever people make a huge to-do list for today then figure out who's going to do it.

Knew the psychic was no good the moment she accepted my cheque.

Vital papers will demonstrate their vitality by moving from where you left them to where you can't find them.

In share trading a bull market is a random market movement causing an investor to mistake himself for a financial genius.

He left his previous job because after they fired him they wouldn't let him stay.

Hell hath no fury like a bureaucrat scorned.

Bet you $4,567.89 you can't guess how much I owe my bookie.

When there's a single thief, it's robbery; when there are a thousand thieves, it's taxation.

Why are mindless people so confident?

Where there's a will, there's an inheritance tax.

Axiom: a market correction invariably occurs the day after you buy shares.

Most dentists are just collectors of old magazines.

All business job descriptions can be written in five words. "Make more money for us."

Hey, CEO, even if it's not your fault, it's your responsibility.

In economics a depression is a period in which you have no belt to tighten.

Always choose a lazy person to do a difficult job because a lazy person will find an easy way to do it. (Bill Gates)

Income tax is the entry fee for the rat race.

It's almost tax season. Anyone have some spare kids?

Let us all be happy and live within our means, even if we have to borrow money to do it.

Whoever said money doesn't grow on trees obviously never sold marijuana.

Whoever said money cannot buy happiness clearly has never paid for a divorce.

70% of accountants do not know what management means, but what is even more scary is that the other 30% do not know what 70% means.

Anyone who thinks money will make you happy hasn't got money.

Money often costs too much. (Ralph Waldo Emerson)

A movie ticket for a baby should cost at least $80.

Money can't buy happiness but it can rent it.

A handful of Nigerian scam artists are wrecking it for all the honest Nigerians who want to wire money to us.

Whenever you hear the word *save*, it is usually the beginning of an advertisement designed to make you spend money.

I see money in your future but it's not yours.

Receipts are just short stories about how stupid you are with money.

There are people who have money and there are people who are rich. (Coco Chanel)

While you'd love to make money at home in your spare time, counterfeiting is harder than you'd think.

To save money on Halloween lollies, set an empty bowl at the front gate and write a nice note that says please only take one lolly. That way everyone can have some.

Budget tip: save money on a bigger TV by simply moving the couch closer to your existing one.

How are poor people so good at finding money for tattoos?

The first people to leave a sinking ship are the strong swimmers.

The two ways of getting on in the world are by one's own industry, or by the ignorance of others.

Doesn't it bother you when you see your tax money wasted on signs telling kangaroos where to cross the road?

I'd like to live as a poor man with lots of money. (Pablo Picasso)

There are more important things in life than money, but the trouble is, they all cost money.

Anybody with money to burn will easily find someone to tend the fire.

It would be nice if the poor got half the money that was spent on studying them.

If money won't make you happy, you won't like poverty either.

I believe in reincarnation so I've left all of my money to myself.

Ninety percent of being an accountant is fighting off the babes.

In most cases being a good boss means hiring talented people and then getting out of their way. (Tina Fey)

Money is not the most important thing in the world. Love is. Fortunately, I love money.

Coin collecting is the only hobby where you end up saving money.

Take away the looks, money, intelligence, charm, charisma and success and, really, there's no difference between you and George Clooney.

If money doesn't bring happiness, pass the money over here. I like to be sad.

Don't keep paying bills. It just encourages them to send more.

A word to the wise is unnecessary; it's the dozy ones who need advice.

She has no desire for money. It's stuff that she wants.

A financial genius is a person who can earn money faster than the family can spend it.

Inflation is being broke with a lot of money in your pocket.

Earn your salary before spending it. (Artemus Ward)

Taxes are never levied for the benefit of the taxed.

Genealogy is a system that traces your family history back as far as your money will go.

A person who makes money hand over foot is called a chiropodist.

Subsidies are devised by politicians to give you back some of your own money in such a way that you are supposed to think it's a gift.

Money isn't everything as long as you have enough.

When a man tells you that he got rich through hard work, ask him whose.

If you're poor you're a hoarder; if you're rich you're a collector.

Turns out that the get rich painfully slowly scheme doesn't work out either.

Some people are so rich they can throw things away that accidentally fall in the toilet.

An economist is someone who gets rich explaining to others why they are poor.

I notice a lot of rich women seeing how small they can get their dogs. (Rita Rudner)

Improve mail delivery - post the posties salary cheque.

Rich people stay rich by living like they are broke and broke people stay broke by living like they are rich.

He was a responsible worker. When anything went wrong, the boss said he was responsible for it.

Ability will get you to the top if the boss has no daughter.

Leaders who don't listen will eventually be surrounded by people who have nothing to say.

Real stupidity beats artificial intelligence every time.

Only one man in a thousand is a leader of men - the other 999 follow women.

First rule of leadership: everything is your fault.

The problem with being a leader is that you're never sure if you're being followed or chased.

Isn't it strange that the same people who laugh at gypsy fortune tellers take economists seriously.

Pay off all your debt and finally getting back to just being broke.

The quickest way to get into debt is to try to keep up with those who are already there.

There has to be a better disaster plan for the company than running round in circles shouting, "What will we do? What will we do?"

Would the Standing Committee please sit down.

After four decimal places, nobody cares.

Saving is a fine thing, especially if your parents have done it for you.

Partying isn't wasting money; rather its investing in good memories.

Public Art is art that is purchased by experts who are not spending their own personal money. (Dave Barry)

Meetings are indispensable when you don't want to do anything.

Showing off is more ridiculous when the thing that is being shown off was bought on credit.

The only important result of a meeting is agreement about next steps.

Ignorance can be educated, crazy can be medicated but there's no cure for stupid.

My bank balance is a constant reminder that I'm safe from identity theft.

THE NONSENSE OF POLITICS

Every few years the Australian politics industry fills the airwaves with the most virulent, scurrilous, wall-to-wall character assassination of nearly every political practitioner in the country - and then declares itself puzzled that Australians have lost trust in its politicians.

Note to politicians and public servants who are on taxpayer-funded expense accounts while travelling.

Expenditures for meals should be limited to the absolute minimum. It should be noted that certain grocery chains often provide free samples of promotional items. Entire meals can be obtained in this manner.

Travellers should also be familiar with indigenous roots, plants and berries. Seek out local knowledge.

If a restaurant must be utilised, travellers should seek "all you can eat" salad bars. This will especially be useful for employees travelling together, as a single plate can feed a whole group.

Employees are also encouraged to bring their own food with them: cans of tuna, spam, and pork and beans can be conveniently consumed at your leisure without the unnecessary bother of heating or costly preparation.

In lieu of extravagant meals, a picnic table can be placed in the parking lot by the dumpster. A garden hose can be made available for liquid refreshment.

A politician visited a village and asked the villagers what their needs were.

"We have two basic needs, honourable sir," replied the village leader. "Firstly, we have a hospital but no doctor.

On hearing this, the politician brought out his mobile phone. After speaking for a while, he told them that there'd be a doctor there tomorrow, and asked for the second problem.

"Secondly, sir, there is no mobile phone coverage anywhere in this village."

⁓

A politician was a guest speaker at the golf club dinner. As he stood up to speak, a few of the men saw it as an opportunity to sneak off to the bar.

An hour later, with the politician still talking, another man joined them. "Is he still talking?" they asked him.

"Yes," the other man answered.

"What on earth is he talking about?"

"I don't know. He's still introducing himself."

⁓

A man and his wife are discussing what they think their son will be when he grows up.

"I have an idea," says the father. He puts a ten-dollar bill, a bottle of whiskey, and a Bible on the coffee table. "If he takes the money, he'll be a banker, if he takes the whiskey, he'll be a wino, and if he takes the Bible, that means he'll be a priest."

So the man and his wife hide just before their son comes in the door, and watch from where they're hiding. The boy saunters over to the coffee table. He picks up the ten-dollar bill, looks at it, then sets it down. He picks up the bottle of whiskey, uncorks it, sniffs it, then sets it down. He picks up the Bible, leafs through it, and sets it down. Then the boy takes the money and stuffs it into his pocket, grabs the whiskey, and walks off with the Bible under his arm.

"Well, how do you like that!" exclaims the father. "He's going to be a politician!"

THE NONSENSE OF POLITICS

Politics is the art of looking for trouble, finding it, misdiagnosing it and then misapplying the wrong remedies. (Mark Twain)

To succeed in politics, it is often necessary to rise above your principles.

That political party is the cream of society - thick, rich and full of clots.

Those who are too smart to engage in politics are punished by being governed by those who are dumber.

Instead of giving a politician the keys to the city, it might be better to change the locks.

If you have been in the Senate since before the internet, get out! The Senate is not a retirement home.

Stop blaming politicians and start blaming the fortune tellers. They knew, and they did nothing.

Politicians have too few morals and ethics to remain lawyers.

One of the penalties for refusing to participate in politics is that you end up being governed by your inferiors. (Plato)

The best thing about this group of political candidates is that only one of them will win.

Politics is when you say you are going to do one thing while intending to do another, then you do neither.

The best argument against democracy is a five-minute conversation with the average voter. (Churchill)

Politicians shake your hand before an election and your confidence after it.

Not all politicians are liars. Some of them actually believe the stupid crap they say.

Why are judges usually lawyers who once knew a politician?

Voting is a process of standing in line for the opportunity to help decide which party will spend your money.

When buying and selling are controlled by legislation, the first things to be bought and sold are legislators. (PJ O'Rourke)

Government is a kind of legalised pillage. Amen.

What Canberra needs is adult supervision.

Statesmen tell you what is true even though it may be unpopular. Politicians will tell you what is popular, even though it may be untrue.

Practical politics consists in ignoring facts.

A promising young man should go into politics so that he can go on promising for the rest of his life.

The more you observe politics, the more you've got to admit that each party is worse than the other.

If I wanted to go crazy I would do it in Canberra because it would not be noticed.

No one party can fool all of the people all of the time; that's why we have two parties.

In politics, an appeaser is one who feeds a crocodile hoping it will eat him last.

A politician is one who is willing to do anything on earth for the workers except become one.

We hang the petty thieves and appoint the great ones to public office. (Aesop)

When the politicians say "every thinking man" they mean themselves, and when candidates appeal to "every intelligent voter" they mean everybody who is going to vote for them.

Support funding the needy but oppose funding the lazy.

Our morbidly obese public service does not need only behaviour modification but bariatric surgery.

History convinces that most bad government results from too much government.

The problem is not that the people are taxed too little. The problem is that government spends too much. (Ronald Reagan)

Why should people be afraid of their governments. Governments should be afraid of their people.

A rule to live by - don't believe anything the government tells you.

A patriot must always be ready to defend his country - against his government.

Don't believe any rumour until the government denies it.

If you put the government in charge of the Sahara Desert, in five years there would be a shortage of sand.

If you think the problems we create are bad, wait until you see our solutions.

Patriotism is supporting your country all the time, and your government when it deserves it.

Politics is a strife of interests masquerading as a contest of principles. (Ambrose Bierce)

It's easier to fool people than to convince them they have been fooled.

Since a politician never believes what he says, he is quite surprised to be taken at his word. (Charles de Gaulle)

Papers say: "Parliament is deadlocked and can't act." That is the greatest blessing that could befall this country.

Democracy is the art and science of running the circus from the monkey cage. (HL Mencken)

Hands up all you people who pay for the free stuff the government gives out.

A recession will never be over until people learn to live with what they've got.

The ballot is stronger than the bullet. (Abraham Lincoln)

Democracy is the process by which people choose the man who'll get the blame.

Nothing is as permanent as a temporary government program.

Nobody spends somebody else's money as carefully as he spends his own.

Know what you own, and know why you own it.

The election is not very far off when a candidate recognises you across the street.

We'd all like to vote for the best person but they are never a candidate.

An honest man in politics shines more there than he would elsewhere. (Mark Twain)

Democracy is the recurrent suspicion that more than half of the people are right more than half the time.

Politics for years has been concerned with right or left instead of right or wrong.

There are always too many Liberal politicians, too many Labor politicians, and never enough Australian politicians.

Electile Dysfunction: the inability to become aroused over any of the choices for Prime Minister put forth by either party.

Since the majority is always wrong, might we try one election day where all the losers take office?

Do you ever get the feeling that the only reason we have elections is to find out if the polls were right? (Robert Orben)

The reason politicians try so hard to get re-elected is that they would hate to have to make a living under the laws they have passed.

Democracy is being allowed to vote for the candidate you dislike least. Sounds familiar.

Why pay money to have your family tree traced; go into politics and your opponents will do it for you warts and all.

Let the people think they govern and they will be governed.

It's dangerous to be right when the government is wrong. (Voltaire)

Politicians lie, even when they're telling the truth.

The Opposition consists of a group of people whose political opinions always manage to keep up with yesterday.

All the taxes paid over a lifetime by the average Australian are spent by the government in less than a second.

Elect a clown. Expect a circus.

Under capitalism, it's dog eat dog. Under communism, it's just the opposite.

Just because you do not take an interest in politics doesn't mean politics won't take an interest in you. (Pericles, 430 BC)

If the government is elected for a second term, think of the mess they'll inherit.

The mystery of government is not how Canberra works but how to make it stop.

A government is the only known vessel that leaks from the top.

A government-funded study has determined that many smokers are ignoring the warning labels on cigarette packages.

Only one thing is impossible for God: to find any sense in most legislation in this country. (Mark Twain)

True terror is to wake up one morning and discover that your high school class mates are running the country.

The real problem with the upcoming election is one of them is going to win.

Give a civil servant a good case and he'll wreck it with clichés, bad punctuation, double negatives, and a convoluted apology.

She always wanted to be a whistleblower but unfortunately she didn't know anything.

Only 9,000 more lies until election day.

Morality: a set of rules laid out by professionals to show the way they would like to act if it was profitable.

When you can't make them see the light, make them feel the heat. (Ronald Reagan)

When the debate is lost, slander becomes the tool of the loser. (Socrates)

Democracy consists of choosing your dictators, after they've told you what you think it is you want to hear.

MARVELLOUS MARRIAGE MEMORIES (INCLUDING FAMILY FAVOURITES)

"Wait a minute! You have been cheating on me all this time!" my wife yelled at me as she found all the letters I had been hiding.

I felt cornered and prepared myself to face her fury, as she got red with anger and started walking towards me. She looked straight into my eyes and gave me a killer look I could never forget.

And that's the last time I played scrabble with her!

As Farmer Brown approached his neighbour's barn, he saw Farmer Jones serenading a tractor with songs and compliments. "What are you doing?" Farmer Brown demanded.

Farmer Jones replied, "My wife and I have been having marital difficulties, and the marital counsellor said I needed to do something sexy to a tractor."

My grandmother told me how she ended up marrying Grandpa. She was in her twenties, and the man she was dating left for war. "We were in love," she recalled, "and wrote to each other every week. It was during that time that I discovered how wonderful your grandfather was."

"Did you marry Grandpa when he came home from the war?" I asked.

"Oh, I didn't marry the man who wrote the letters. Your grandfather was the mailman."

After Adam stayed out late a few nights. Eve became suspicious.

"You're running around with another woman, admit it!" she demanded.

"What other woman?" Adam shot back. "You're it!"

That night, Adam was fast asleep when he was awakened by Eve poking him in the chest.

"What are you doing?"

"Counting your ribs."

A wife is scrambling eggs when her husband bursts into the kitchen.

"Careful," he cries. "Careful! You're cooking too many at once. Too many! Scramble them! Now! We need more butter. They're going to stick! Careful! Now scramble them again! Hurry up! Are you crazy? Don't forget to salt them. You know you always forget to salt them. Use the salt. Use the salt! The salt!"

The wife turns and asks, "What is wrong with you?"

Her husband calmly replies, "I wanted to show you what it feels like when I'm driving."

My mum told me the best time to ask my dad for anything was during sex. Not the best advice I'd ever been given but I burst in through the bedroom door saying, "Can I have a new bike?" He was very upset. His secretary was surprisingly nice about it. I got the bike.

"Cash, cheque or charge?" I asked, after folding items the woman wished to purchase.

As she fumbled for her wallet, I noticed a remote control for a television set in her purse.

"So, do you always carry your TV remote?" I asked.

"No," she replied, "but my husband refused to come shopping with me, and I figured this was the most evil thing I could do to him legally."

MARVELLOUS MARRIAGE MEMORIES (INCLUDING FAMILY FAVOURITES)

If a marriage is supposed to be 50/50, why isn't it okay for the husband to raise the toilet seat and the wife to lower it?

Just think, if it weren't for marriage, men would go through life thinking they had no faults at all.

Love may be blind but marriage is a real eye-opener.

A good marriage is one where each partner secretly suspects they got the better deal.

Marriage is just a fancy word for adopting an overgrown male child who cannot be handled by his parents anymore.

In our marriage everything is 50/50. I cook, he eats. I wash, he wears. I shop, he pays!

Marriage is just your spouse always standing in front of the drawer or cabinet you want to open.

The secret for a happy marriage remains a secret.

Love: a temporary insanity cured by marriage. (Ambrose Bierce)

It has been established that 62% of marriage conversation is just spouses stating, "I never said that."

The boring thing about "No sex before marriage" is that kids will never get to attend their parents' wedding.

Your marriage is in trouble if your wife says, "You're only interested in one thing," and you can't remember what it is.

Marriage counselling is where you learn you're not the only person your spouse won't listen to.

At this point in the marriage, showering together is just a convenient way to check for ticks and sun spots.

Life after death is as improbable as sex after marriage.

We interrupt this marriage to bring you the football season.

"Until Death Do Us Part" was put into marriage vows when the life expectancy was thirty-five. Needs a rethink.

Marriage is wanting to share your entire life with someone who'll leave you alone.

Makeup tip - you aren't in the circus.

A grandmother is a babysitter who watches the kids instead of the television.

Tupperware is a fun way to store your leftovers until you throw them away.

If the marriage counsellor asks how long since you've had sex, she means with your spouse. Learn from my mistakes.

Marital Bliss Review: the length of a marriage is inversely proportional to the amount spent on the wedding.

God created sex. Priests created marriage. (Voltaire)

Anyone remember as a kid, on finishing your meal having to ask your parents, "May I leave the table please?"

Marry someone who laughs at the same things you do.

Buy a motor home. The kids won't move back if they cannot find you.

Young children have a unique superpower: place a toddler in a queen-sized bed and they will find a sleeping position that ensures no one else can fit in there with them.

One should always be in love. That is the reason one should never marry. (Oscar Wilde)

When you see what some women marry, you realise how they must hate to work for a living.

If your husband is having a bad day, surprise, so will you.

Remember only having three TV channels to choose from and you were the remote?

Out of the mouths of babes come things parents never should have said.

Dressing a baby is like putting an octopus into a string bag, making sure none of the arms hang out.

Don't buy one of those baby intercoms. Babies pretend to be dead. They're bastards, and they do it on purpose.

He wanted to have a baby for about five years, but she wants one forever.

Marry someone who can cook. Looks go away but hunger doesn't.

Two golden rules for a happy marriage: 1. The wife is always right. 2. When you feel she is wrong, slap yourself and read Rule No.1 again.

He's so lazy, he'd marry a pregnant woman.

Men are simple things. They can survive a whole weekend with only three things: beer, boxer shorts and batteries for the remote control.

Men chase women they have no intention of marrying following the same urge that makes dogs chase cars they have no intention of driving.

Girls have an unfair advantage over men: if they can't get what they want by being smart, they can get it by being dumb. (Yul Brynner)

Why didn't someone speak up at my wedding? Bastards!

The ideal man doesn't smoke, doesn't drink, doesn't do drugs, doesn't swear, doesn't get angry, doesn't exist.

Anyone who says their wedding day was the best day of their life has never experienced two Snickers falling down at the same time from a vending machine

Sorry for writing "Everyone makes mistakes" in your wedding guestbook.

Raised four daughters with only one bathroom and still there was love.

For an additional $4.95 we'll supply a receipt that matches what you told your spouse you paid.

My wife has just spent $6,000 on a new motorcycle for me as a surprise gift. I was speechless so I rushed off to the shops straight away and bought her a lovely new steam iron. You can't do enough for a good woman.

Sometimes, when two people love each other very much, they get married and ruin everything.

Ten percent of women think their ass is too skinny, 30% think their ass is too fat and 60% say they don't care; they love him, he's a good man and they wouldn't trade him for the world.

When two people love each other deeply, nothing is impossible. Except deciding on where to eat.

We've decided we don't want children and we'll be telling them at dinner tonight.

The best time to give advice to your children is while they're still young enough to believe you know what you're talking about.

Children would do house cleaning if the spray bottles made laser-gun sounds.

As a child my family's menu consisted of two choices: take it or leave it.

He was raised as an only child, which really annoyed his sister.

Never marry a woman who was captain of the debating team. You do so at your own peril.

English lesson for children: tell them every time they use an apostrophe to make a word plural, a puppy dies.

The best way to keep children at home is to make the home atmosphere pleasant, and let the air out of their tyres.

Well at least he has finally found his true love ... What a pity he can't marry himself. (Frank Sinatra)

If you want your children to listen just talk quietly to someone else.

Don't trust your children. They are here to replace us.

A good neighbour doesn't borrow his garden tools back too often.

Teenagers have to realise that the day will come when they'll know as little as their parents.

The wife told him to go to the doctors and get some of those tablets that "help get an erection". You should have seen her face when he came back and tossed her some diet pills. He's still looking for a place to live.

She loved all mythical creatures: vampires, unicorns, werewolves, kids who listen.

How do we no longer have enough hangers for the clothes we washed that were on hangers before we wore them?

Why it is that only adults have difficulty with child-proof bottles?

No one ever died from sleeping in an unmade bed. I have known mothers who remake the bed after their children do it because there is wrinkle in the spread or the blanket is on crooked. This is sick. (Erma Bombeck)

Grandchildren cannot understand that when you were their age television was called books.

Children get their energy by draining it from their parents.

Wish my siblings would stop calling me "spoiled" just because I'm the youngest in the family. My parents just kept having children until they got one they liked.

Grandchildren are their grandparents' toys.

How come finishing my food is going to save a starving child in Africa?

The appeal of being a nudist is apparent every washing day.

When a child says, "I want Mummy," that's their version of, "I want to speak to your supervisor."

Letting your child "help" you is the quickest way for you to learn you are a control freak.

To get children to keep their feet on the ground, put some responsibility on their shoulders.

When a mother tells her child they can be anyone they want to be, they are suggesting identity theft.

Always read your partner's horoscope to see what kind of day you're going to have.

If you have kids you can check your pulse using the veins on the side of your head.

Frugal people, before sending their pyjamas to the laundry, stuff a sock in each pocket.

Remember tucking your children in bed and saying, "See you in the morning!" and then seeing them twenty-one more times before sunrise?

My wife, she's carrying our first child. He's eight, the lazy little ...

Don't be discouraged if your children reject your advice; years later they will offer it to their offspring.

The only reason they say "women and children first" is to test the strength of the lifeboats. (Jean Kerr)

Those who think your children are good know nothing of the dark side.

Only a few years ago, the average parents had four children. Nowadays, the average child has four parents.

One day you'll be able to tell your grandchildren you survived the great toilet paper shortage of 2020.

Today's children would be less spoiled if we could spank grandparents.

According to customer service, the TV repairman should be here sometime between 10:00 am and the return of Christ.

Millennials will laugh when you tell them you have only twenty-two photos of your entire childhood.

Don't bungee jump. Chances are you were born because of broken rubber and you don't want to die the same way.

She said, "When I grow old I don't want people saying 'That sweet old lady ...' I want them saying, 'Oh crap, what's she up to now?'"

Stay positive, ladies. Maybe he just didn't hear you the first one hundred times.

The secret of dealing successfully with a child is not to be its parent.

About age thirty most women think about having children; most men think about dating them.

Mothers are more fond of their children than fathers because mothers are more certain the children are their own. (Aristotle)

Have your children while your parents are still young enough to take care of them.

Childproofing your home will not work because the kids will still get in.

How is it that farmers can lose money every year, live well, educate their children, and then die rich?

Grandparents are those who think your children are wonderful even though they're sure you're not raising them right.

Childbirth is when you get to go through thirty-six hours of contractions; he gets to hold your hand and say, "focus ... breathe ... push ..." while you scream, "You did this to me, you bastard!"

A lady inserted an ad in the classifieds: "Husband Wanted". Next day she received a hundred letters all saying the same thing: "You can have mine."

Let's join our hands together and pray for my husband who very tragically compared me to his ex.

Oh, what a tangled web do parents weave when they think that their children are naive. (Ogden Nash)

All husbands lie on their tax returns by listing themselves as head of household.

A good husband makes a good wife.

Why does a woman work for ten years to change her husband and then complain he is not the man she married?

A women's work that is never done is the stuff that she has asked her husband to do.

A good wife always forgives her husband when she's wrong.

I was nauseous and tingly all over. I was either in love or I had smallpox. (Woody Allen)

Cosmetics are a boon to every woman, but a girl's best friend is still a nearsighted man.

Nursing mother tip: do not nurse a child who wears braces.

Any woman wanting a husband never had one before.

Honey, I know where everything is in this house because I live here -- said no husband ever.

How many husbands have I had? Do you mean apart from my own? (Zsa Zsa Gabor)

Nine out of ten husbands agree that their wife is always right. The tenth husband has not been seen since the survey was conducted.

To get back at your husband, just pour some water on the floor in front of the washing machine and look at him spending two plus hours to try and fix it.

Bridge: probably the only time in which a wife is always eager to do her husband's bidding.

A daughter is someone who Dad likes because she reminds him why he married his wife, and who Mum is afraid of because she reminds her of why her husband married her.

A tip for husbands: "You can't expect me to remember your birthday when you never look any older."

I told my wife to embrace her mistakes. And she hugged me.

A man should never plant a garden larger than his wife can take care of.

When your wife gets a little upset, just remember a simple "calm down" in a soothing voice is all it takes to get her a lot more upset.

When your wife is mowing the lawn that is not the best time to ask her when dinner will be ready.

It takes a lot of courage for a man to admit his wife is wrong.

I am his *awfully wedded* wife. (Jane Ace)

Whenever my wife says, "I've just been thinking", it means I have to move, build, paint or buy something.

My wife is singing in the house so I'm sitting outside so the neighbours don't think I'm hitting her.

My wife is blaming me for ruining her birthday, which is ridiculous because I didn't even know it was her birthday.

If his wife ends an argument with "Fine, do what you want!" he's pretty sure the words "If you do, I'll stab you in your sleep." are implied.

I told my wife she was putting her eyebrows too high. She looked surprised.

After an argument with my wife I tighten all the lids on the jars. Just so I can say, "Oh, so you need me now?"

Never, ever explain to your wife that it's the washer and dryer that actually does the laundry.

Told my wife I wanted our kids every other weekend and she reminded me that we're married and live together, so I'd have to see them every day.

My wife and I tried for a long time to have kids. Nearly twelve minutes one night.

Fathers Day is just like Mothers Day, only you don't spend as much.

There's nothing I've learned from being a father that I couldn't just as easily have figured out from setting all my money on fire.

It's much easier to become a father than to be one.

For you PC tragics pushing for "Fathers Day" to be called "Special Person's Day", you already have a day of your own. It's April 1st.

A first-grader handed his teacher a note from his mother. The note read, "The opinions expressed by this child are not necessarily those of his parents."

A little girl had just finished her first week of school. "I'm just wasting my time," she said to her mother. "I can't read, I can't write, and they won't let me talk!"

How did we survive? Our mothers wiped our faces with spit on a hanky not an antibacterial wipe.

Despite the old saying of never take your troubles to bed, some women still sleep with their husbands.

Four-year-old boy said when he grew up he wanted to be like his daddy, but mother said he couldn't do both.

The phrase "working mother" is redundant.

He had bad luck with both of his wives. The first one left him, and the second one didn't.

Thanks to whoever explained to my mother that WTF stood for "Wow That's Fantastic". Her texts are a lot more fun now.

Peeing on a stick is one of the first disgusting things you'll have to do as a mother.

When I asked my mother if I was adopted, she said, "Not yet, but we placed an ad."

The most remarkable thing about my mother is that for thirty years she served the family nothing but leftovers. The original meal has never been found.

They all want to save the earth but not one of them wants to help their mother do the dishes.

Mothers know more about chaos theory than most physicists.

Ever since my nan heard about the dangers of using dirty needles she's been too scared to go near her knitting.

Major cause of divorce is thermostat wars, not infidelity or finances.

They divorced because squeezing the toothpaste tube in the middle is unforgivable.

She considered being a stay-at-home mum until she realised the kids would be there.

Going out is good ... Coming home is even better.

His divorce came as a complete surprise. That's what happens when you haven't been home in eighteen years.

Your ex asking to be friends after getting a divorce is like ... kidnappers asking to "keep in touch" after letting you go.

Divorce means no longer having to pretend you like your in-laws.

Just another of our many disagreements. He wants a no-fault divorce, whereas I would prefer to have the bastard crucified. (JB Handelsman)

Many a person would get a divorce if they could do it without making their partner happy.

Only put off until tomorrow what you are willing to die having left undone.

Behavioural disorders used to be called being a little brat.

Children are morning people, especially on December 25th.

I married beneath me. All women do. (Nancy Astor)

To encourage your children, remember the longer the string the higher the kites will fly.

At every party there are two kinds of people - those who want to go home and those who don't. The trouble is, they are usually married to each other.

Married couples do it about seventy-four times per year. It's the end of November now, so it seems I'm going to have a seriously exciting December!

Getting married at eighteen sounds a lot like leaving a party at 9:00 pm.

Bridge is a friendly game invented by two married couples who disliked each other.

A year is the exact length of time that will pass from the day you get married to the day you forget your first anniversary.

Because of quarantine, many parents are about to discover that the teacher was not the problem.

Hearsay: what toddlers do when anyone mutters a dirty word.

Always check the height of nearby ceiling fans before giving a toddler a ride on your shoulders. How I learned this rule is not important.

The little girl staring at a pair of false teeth soaking in a glass whispered, "The tooth fairy will never believe this!"

Happiness is having a loving, caring close-knit family - in another city. (George Burns)

Want to call a family meeting? Just turn off the wi-fi and wait in the room where it is located.

Have you ever taken something out of the clothes hamper because it had become, relatively, the cleanest thing?

Sorry, but your kids don't look adorable when they lose their teeth; they look like tiny homeless people.

The worst thing about spanking a kid in K-Mart is that I have no idea who's kid this is.

We have two kids right now and we support adoption. Just pay the shipping and handling and you can have them.

Don't be ashamed of who you are; that's your parents' job.

In a well-ordered universe camping would take place indoors.

Shop local because Amazon will not support your children's cricket team.

The collective noun for a group of kids is "migraine".

Adulting is putting back a pack of chicken for $8.58 because you see one for $8.17.

Son, don't worry. If you are ever kidnapped they'll bring you back.

Forty years ago the "parental control" button was a belt.

"One man's trash is another man's treasure" is a wonderful saying, but a horrible way to find out you were adopted.

Anyone else afraid of a world run by adults who were never spanked as kids and got trophies just for participating?

If you are not yelling at your kids, you are not spending enough time with them.

If you ask what our baby's name is he hasn't told us yet.

It's so hot we have the air conditioner set on bankruptcy.

Too busy trying to keep up with the laundry to worry about keeping up with the Joneses.

My parents never allowed violent video games. Just family-friendly board games with questions like, "Who murdered this guy with a metal pipe?"

Confuse your kids by telling them that you are older than the internet.

A pretty important part of being a dad is waiting in the car.

Silence is golden unless you have kids; then it is just downright suspicious.

The longer I stay at home, the more homeless I look.

The hardest job kids face today is learning good manners without seeing any. (Fred Astaire)

Having kids is like continually cleaning up after a huge party that you didn't attend.

HOUSEHOLD TIPS

The only advantage of not being too good a housekeeper is that your guests are so pleased to feel how very much better they are than you.

A house is just a place to keep your stuff while you go out and get more stuff.

People who live in stone houses shouldn't throw glasses.

Hurry up and clean the house; we don't want people to think we live like we actually live.

Just spent the past hour chasing a daddy long legs around my house until I realised it was just a crack in my glasses.

If doing the same thing over and over again and expecting a different result is the definition of insanity, I'll stop cleaning the house.

Aggressive? He could start an argument in an empty house.

Ever been trapped in the corner of your shower because the cold water is running when someone elsewhere in the house turned a tap on?

The day I worry about cleaning my house is the day they come out with a ride-on vacuum cleaner.

There's no real need to do housework - after four years it doesn't get any worse. (Quentin Crisp)

Most ladies agree: housekeeping is like being caught in a revolving door.

Household hint: do all of your ironing in the dryer.

True friendship is when you walk into their house and your wi-fi connects automatically.

Stevie Wonder's housekeepers probably don't do a damn thing all day long.

Having meetings at my house for people with OCD, and if anyone feels the urge to tidy up, by all means go ahead.

We've got stained glass windows in our house; it's those damned pigeons.

She was Home Schooled Valedictorian!

It's a downer when you post a photo of your clean home and it is flagged and then removed as fake news.

Bliss is finding a shirt right side out when folding it.

What's going on? It's two days until Christmas and none of the stores have their Valentine's Day stuff displayed.

Microwave minutes are longer than normal minutes.

Apologising for not having cleaned is easier than cleaning. (Sarah Millican)

There is always more dirty laundry than clean laundry.

Untidy? I had to clean my house for two hours just to tell guests, "Sorry about the mess."

Childhood is like being drunk. Everyone remembers what you did, except you.

The first person you should be careful not to fool is yourself. Because you are the easiest person to fool.

Gardening observation: a weed is a plant that has mastered every survival skill except for learning how to grow in rows.

Killer tip: photoshop a cleaner house into the background of your photos.

Gardening requires lots of water - most of it in the form of perspiration.

Gardening is cheaper than therapy and you get tomatoes.

Gardening tip: remember, when you bury a body, cover it with endangered plants so it is illegal to dig it up.

As you know, an expensive plant is something that dies if you don't water it, and rots if you do.

I don't think of myself as having a "grey" thumb. Rather as a plant hospice worker, easing the transition of plants so they can go to Jesus.

What do gardeners do when they retire?

Gardeners understand that more dirt comes out of a hole than they can get back into it.

Axiom: your lawn is always slightly bigger than your desire to mow it.

ROMANCE AND ROMANTIC NOTIONS

A gynaecologist notices that a new patient is nervous. While putting on the latex gloves, he asks her if she knows how they make latex gloves. The patient says no.

The doctor says, "There is a plant in China full of latex that people of various hand sizes dip their hands into and let them dry."

She does not crack a smile, but later she laughs. The doctor says, "What's so funny?"

She says, "I'm imagining how they make condoms."

~

Grandma and Granddad were visiting their kids overnight. When Granddad found a bottle of Viagra in his son's medicine cabinet, he asked about using one of the pills.

The son said, "I don't think you should take one, Dad. They're very strong and very expensive."

"How much?" asked Granddad.

"$10.00 a pill." answered the son.

"I don't care," said Granddad, "I'd still like to try one, and before we leave in the morning, I'll put the money under the pillow."

Later the next morning, the son found $110 under the pillow. He called Granddad and said, "I told you each pill was $10, not $110. "

"I know," said Granddad. "The hundred is from Grandma."

~

A few months after his parents were divorced, little Johnny passed by his mom's bedroom and saw her lying on her bed and moaning, "I need a man, I need a man!"

Over the next couple of months, he saw her doing this several times. One day, he came home from school and heard her moaning. When he peeked into her bedroom, he saw a naked man with her.

Little Johnny ran into his room, took off his clothes, threw himself on his bed, and began moaning, "Ohh, I need a bike! I need a bike!"

Which reminds me of the three women playing golf at the Redcliffe Golf Club, when a well endowed streaker race across the fairway in front of the ladies with only a cover over his head.

One lady said, "Well I never! I have been mislead to believe that this is an exclusive members only club ".

The second lady said, "Well he is certainly not my husband."

And the third lady said, "I can assure you he is not a member of this club."

A young man goes in search of his first condom and asks the assistant about the different packages.

"The two pack is for the weekend warrior, one for Friday night and one for Saturday night. The eight pack is for the active guy, one for every day of the week and twice on Sunday.

The twelve pack is for married people. One for January, one for February, and so on."

Competition to write a short, short story which contains religion, sex and mystery. Winner's story: "Oh God, I am pregnant. I wonder who did it."

I asked a Chinese girl for her number.

She said, "Sex! Sex! Sex! Free sex tonight!"

I said, "Wow!"

Then her friend said, "She means 666-3629."

ROMANCE AND ROMANTIC NOTIONS

Husband got excited thinking she was touching herself under the covers, but she was just actually just opening a Kit Kat and didn't want to share.

Ladies, if you think husbands aren't good listeners, whisper "Come here, I'm naked" from anywhere in the house and see what happens.

Her husband tried to embarrass her in front of his friends by saying she wasn't any good in bed, but he was shocked when his friends disagreed.

Sex with human, OK. Sex with cow, not OK. Grabbing cow titty, OK. Grabbing Karen in accounting's titty, not OK. Apparently.

It could be worse. What if sex was fattening?

According to the Australian Bureau of Statistics, there are 18,346 people involved in sex right now. There is one poor person reading this one liner. You hang in there.

If you think men are the stronger sex, watch a man react when the girlfriend says, "What did you just say to me?"

If a woman was pregnant for two years, whatever she gave birth to would not be afraid of the dark.

Seeing a mattress on top of a car, could it be a prostitute making house calls?

Apparently an infection with Covid causes loss of taste. Looking back at my exes I must have been infected for years.

After all these years of impotence, on my headstone I want it to read, "Stiff At Last."

The real power of a man is the size of the smile on the woman sitting next to him.

If it's your birthday in November, then you know your parents really enjoyed Valentine's Day.

This pregnancy test confirmed her worst fear. She was just fat.

You know your relationship is in trouble when she loads her vibrator with batteries from your pacemaker.

She came home with a vibrator, started waving it about and screamed at me, "I don't need you now! I don't need you now!" but guess who had to put the batteries in!

The only thing the lady wanted negative in her life was pregnancy tests.

If pregnancy were a book they would cut the last two chapters. (Norah Ephron)

Nausea, bloating, pelvic pain, acne, insomnia, fatigue, facial hair, bleeding gums, backaches; yes, pregnancy is wonderful.

When life closes a door, just open it again. That's how doors work.

A nice girl is one who whispers sweet nothing-doings in your ear.

He felt very humble but had the strength to fight it.

A false pregnancy can be considered labouring under a misconception.

Anyone have an owner's manual for a husband, because mine makes a whining sound?

At my age, safe sex means only sleeping with women who know CPR.

Guys are at their mathematical best when a girl says she is pregnant.

A push-up bra is to a woman's chest what "breathing-in" is to a man's stomach.

I went to buy some condoms today, and I said to the pharmacist, "Excuse me, I need some condoms." And he said, "Just a minute." And I said, "Oh, how did you know that's my brand?"

Saw the neighbour's kid trying to spray whipped cream on his cat, so thinking he overheard something last night in that house he wasn't supposed to.

Prescription: a physician's guess at what will best prolong the situation with least harm to the patient. (Ambrose Bierce)

The best thing about Valentine's Day is when it's over.

Why would you clone people when you can go to bed with them and make a baby? C'mon, it's stupid. (Ray Bradbury)

Treat her like a queen and she'll treat you like a king. Treat her like a game and she'll show you how it's played - to your sorrow.

If women are always right, why do they always pick wrong men?

Those hot pants of hers were so damned tight, I could hardly breathe. (Benny Hill)

She looked like an apple turnover that got crushed in a grocery bag on a hot day.

Don't get excited. A trail of clothes leading to my bedroom means that I dropped them on the way from the dryer. That's all.

Thingy: Female interpretation: Any part under a car's hood; Male interpretation: The strap fastener on a woman's bra.

The push-up bra is the strangely acceptable female equivalent of a rolled up sock stuffed in men's underwear.

Just slung my bra off and threw it on the couch where there are already two other bras, so if my maths is right, it's Wednesday.

The only really firm rule of cross dressing is that neither sex should ever wear anything they haven't yet figured out how to go to the bathroom in. (PJ O'Rourke)

Having sex is like doing fractions in maths. It's improper for the larger one to be on top.

Silence doesn't mean your sexual performance left her speechless.

Just before we have sex, the question often is: to pee, or not to pee?

Literature is mostly about having sex and not much about having children; life is the other way around.

They'd been married for fifteen years today, so went down to the local registry office to renew their vows of celibacy to each other.

Forget sexy. Can someone bring back intelligence?

Thou shalt not commit adultery; now, you know no guy would have ever dreamed that one up.

Restaurant toilets are so dangerous. So many of his first-time dates have gone there and never come back.

There is an element of seduction in shoes that doesn't exist for men. A woman can be sexy, charming, witty or shy just with her shoes.

I once had a pornographic book that was printed in Braille. I used to rub the dirty parts. (Woody Allen)

Some are too shy to express their sexual needs except over the phone to people they don't know.

Sexual harassment can be a touchy subject.

Watching a baby being born is a little like watching a wet St Bernard coming in through the cat door. (Jeff Foxworthy)

The smaller the breasts, the better the eye contact.

Viagra before going to sleep at least stops you falling out of bed.

There is a correlation between the number of days since a man last had sex, and the number of things that he is willing to do for a woman.

Sex: the pleasure is momentary, the position ridiculous, and the expense damnable. (Lord Chesterfield)

Be naughty - save Santa a trip.

Men are like portable heaters that snore. (Rita Rudner)

Fishing is like dating. It's all catch and release until you find a keeper.

May the shooter's seventy-two virgins be all males.

In vitro fertilisation is the inoculate conception.

Eunuchs are cut off from temptation.

Does the term "cul-de-sac" always make anyone else think of a scrotum?

A penis is part of the male anatomy which contains the brain.

For most one-night stands, thirty minutes is plenty time enough.

Everything a hermaphrodite says is a case of he said, she said.

We had different ideas as to what the problem was: she bought me Viagra; I bought her a treadmill.

Don't use a paediatrician who isn't a parent.

He was bisexual. Had sex twice a year.

Some people think having large breasts makes a woman stupid. Actually, it's quite the opposite: a woman having large breasts makes men stupid.

Men are those creatures with two legs and eight hands. (Jayne Mansfield)

If he only wants you for your breasts, legs, and thighs, send him to KFC.

There are three reasons for breastfeeding: the milk is always at the right temperature; it comes in attractive containers; and the cat can't get it.

It has been reported that women have one breast bigger than the other. Or is that just bollocks?

An inch is a unit of measurement whose length is consistently underestimated by men.

When I was young I used to poke holes in my parent's condoms so that there could be someone else to do the dishes.

If you touch me I won't be responsible for your injuries.

She switched her sister's tampons with party poppers. Obviously the sister does not have a sense of humour.

Pyrex is the star sign for a test tube baby.

The weaker sex is the stronger because of the weakness of the stronger sex for the weaker sex.

Women reach their sexual peak after thirty-five years; men reach theirs after about three minutes.

He hasn't had sex for about one year, four months, twenty-four days and fifty-six minutes, but it doesn't bother him.

Put bubble wrap under the mattress during sex and it sounds like fireworks - makes for much more festive mood.

To succeed with the opposite sex, just tell her you're impotent and she can't wait to disprove it. (Cary Grant)

When will we have a television show that says, "You will be delighted to know that this program contains strong sexual content?"

I would rather cuddle then have sex. If you are good with grammar you will get it.

Halloween is easily the scariest night of the year, what with the dead rising from their graves and fat girls thinking they look sexy dressed as cats.

Murder is a crime, but describing murder is not; sex is not a crime, but describing sex is.

Of course we gays dress well. We didn't spend all that time in the closet doing nothing.

It doesn't matter if you're black or white, heterosexual or homosexual, man or woman, because cats hate all of you.

A man will fantasise that he's having sex with ***someone*** else; a woman will fantasise she's having sex with ***anyone*** else. (Jo Brand)

The arrival of pubic hair means: "Welcome to the prime of your life." The arrival of ear hair means: "Thanks for playing."

Men think about sex every seven seconds. The rest of the time is spent trying to come up with a lie when a woman asks, "What are you thinking?"

During sex you burn as many calories as running 8 km. Who runs 8 km in 30 seconds?

In a bizarre turn of events, erectile dysfunction cases are on the rise.

After taking a sexual harassment course he thought he'd be pretty good at it.

Amnesia is a condition that enables a woman who has gone through labour to have sex again.

The word "darling" is the popular form of address used in speaking to a member of the opposite sex whose name you cannot at the moment remember.

Courtship is a period during which a girl decides whether or not she can do better.

Sexual freedom for some people means the freedom from having to have sex.

Because of the sexual revolution, kids today will grow up and never know what "dirty" means.

A tomboy is a bisexual girl's dream lover. (Mokokoma Mokhonoana)

Three stages of sex in a man's life: tri weekly, try weekly, and try weakly.

It's called PMS because that is easier to say than oestrogen induced manic depressive bipolar disorder prone to fits of psychopathic rage.

Flirting is making a baby step for baby-making steps.

The difference between flirting and sexual harassment - if you're attractive it's flirting.

In the past, safe sex meant not being caught.

If average adults have sex fifty-four times a year, this should be a heck of a three months.

If love is the answer, could you rephrase the question?

New club for condom lovers is "Members Only".

Love is only a dirty trick played on us to achieve continuation of the species. (Somerset Maughan)

Do you believe in love at first sight or should I walk by again?

It was love at first sight until I took a second look.

Politeness has become so rare that people mistake it for flirtation.

If you love someone, set them free; then text them fifty times a day, telling them how much you love them and how they're now free.

Looking for love? It's on page 357, bottom right, in Webster's Dictionary.

I've been told that I'm a great listener by several women, a majority of whom have lovely boobs.

Ever had this fantasy to make love to two women ... like, in the same year?

Why is it only my wife who tells me that "it's the little things in life that matter"?

After clearing your browser history do a quick Google search for things like "Feeding the hungry" and "How to thank a loving wife".

He asked his wife, "Last night, were you faking it?" She said, "No, I was really sleeping."

If you get an e-mail from a "bored housewife thirty-four, looking for some action!", send her some ironing. That'll keep her busy.

Have a tremendous sex drive as my girlfriend lives eighty kilometres away

Husband challenges his wife to tell him something that will make him both happy and sad at the same time. She thinks about it for a moment and then responds, "Your penis is bigger than your brother's."

Life is too short. Buy the damn shoes!

If you were born in September, it's pretty safe to assume that your parents started their new year with a bang.

People think I hate sex. I don't. I just don't like things that stop you from seeing the television properly. (Victoria Wood)

There is a DVD on how to improve your foreplay. Suggest you fast-forward through the boring bit at the beginning.

I hate it when people radiotype us blondes as dumb.

He thought there was something wrong with his testicles. One is bigger than the other two.

Men wear the pants in a relationship, but women control the zipper.

You are my favourite cardio workout. Nudge, nudge.

He heard that alcohol and sunlight will kill the Covid virus, so if you see him naked on the front lawn, he's doing medical research.

My husband asked me why I watch cooking shows when I can't cook, so I asked him why he bothered watching porn.

He's got a dig bick. You read that wrong.

When a man brings his wife flowers for no reason, there's a reason.

Golf is almost like sex. It's still fairly good even when it's bad.

Sex without love is simply healthy exercise. (Robert A Heinlein)

Confidence is the sexiest thing a woman can wear.

Although I'm eighty I still chase women. But only downhill.

Men, don't judge women by kilos, and you won't be judged by centimetres.

Women who do not play hard to get are hard to get.

Men say women should come with instructions. Hello! When was the last time you saw a bloke read instructions?

She has been upgraded to Santa's naughty list - Platinum member.

Max Factor mascara makes eyelashes appear three times longer? Max Factor should make condoms.

Well-behaved women rarely make history. (Marilyn Monroe)

Women who say the quickest way to a man's heart is through his stomach haven't seen his browser history.

You know you've had good sex when you walk outside and the neighbours are clapping.

It's the invention of clothes, not nature, that made "private parts" private.

She wanted to be the reason he looked down at his phone and smiled.

She looked under her bed in case there was a man there. Well, you never knew your luck.

Yes I do specialise in maths. Ladies, please form a y = mx+c.

I like threesomes with two women, not because I'm a cynical sexual predator but because I'm a romantic. I'm looking for "The One". And I'll find her more quickly if I audition two at a time. (Russell Brand)

When I'm good, I'm very good, but when I'm bad, I'm better. (Mae West)

How would you like your eggs in the morning? Unfertilised.

Don't have sex with the windows open. Love may be blind but the neighbours aren't.

If you have sex with a stranger and wake up not knowing their name, take them to Starbucks and check the name on their cup of coffee.

No, son, it was Lebanese food we had last night, not lesbian.

She hates shopping for bras. You would think with the growing population of aging baby boomers, they would have more of a selection in thirty-six long.

Despite what women say, boobs are proof that blokes can focus on two things at once.

A recent study concluded that staring at women's boobs for ten minutes a day increases life expectancy, said the 123-year-old gentleman.

She wished cake went straight to her boobs.

It's only fair to throw Monopoly money at strippers with fake boobs.

I have no objection to anyone's sex life as long as they don't practise it in the street and frighten the horses. (Oscar Wilde)

He was beaten up by a busty woman in an elevator when staring at her boobs and she said, "Would you please press 1?" So he did. He doesn't remember much afterwards.

She swore there was a black hole between her boobs because when she dropped something there it was gone for good.

Please move your boobs away from the sunlight. I hate the smell of burning plastic.

Girls, if a bloke interrupts his video game to text you back, marry him.

Health advice: don't let your affection give you an infection so put some protection on that erection.

Hey, erectile dysfunction pill maker, I am really not up for four hours of anything. Do you have something in the twenty-minute range?

Better sexy and racy, than sexist and racist. (Stephen Fry)

Note to philanderers: wear shirts with lipstick-coloured collars.

Flowers say, "I'm sorry." Diamonds say, "I've learned my lesson."

Physics is like sex: sure, it may give some practical results, but that's not why we do it. (Richard Feynman, theoretical physicist)

They say if the palm of your hand itches, you're going to get something, and if your crotch itches, you've already got it.

Women with "pasts" interest men because men hope that history will repeat itself. (Mae West)

What men want in a relationship is to be really, really close to someone who will leave them alone.

If high heels were so wonderful, men would still be wearing them.

A mime artist assaulted a lady yesterday - the bastard did things that were unspeakable.

Brevity is the soul of lingerie. (Dorothy Parker)

Ladies, wearing makeup during a heat wave makes you look like a Picasso painting.

The proper skirt length is six centimetres below your cellulite.

My washer and dryer finished at the same time, but I think my dryer faked it.

None of her yoga pants have ever been to yoga.

My boyfriend and I live together, which means we don't have sex - ever. Now that the milk is free, we've both become lactose intolerant. (Margaret Cho)

Laundry: washing, thirty minutes; drying, forty minutes; putting away, 5–8 business days.

Little girls like dolls, little boys like soldiers, but big girls like soldiers and big boys like dolls.

Cinderella is proof that a fancy pair of shoes can change your life.

Ladies, if you are tired of your man complaining about how long it takes you to get ready, start blow drying your hair in the nude. No more complaints.

I'm a heroine addict. I need to have sex with women who have saved someone's life. (Mitch Hedberg)

Fashion tip for young ladies: cut the swooshes off Nike socks and use as eyebrows.

Ladies, the counter to a bad-hair day is to wear a low-cut blouse.

In twenty years our country will be run by people who were homeschooled by day drinkers.

Nothing is really lost until your mum cannot find it.

A new study has found that men have a hard time reading women's facial expressions because they usually aren't looking at her face.

Whoever said "All men are created equal" obviously has never been to a nude beach.

New survey: 55% of men expect to pay on the first date, while the other 45% have never been on a second date.

To come across as younger than they are: women buy creams that promise to slow aging; men buy fast cars. (Mokokoma Mokhonoana)

Women use twice as many words per day as men because they have to repeat everything they say to them.

All men are convinced that all women suffer from Attention-To-Their-Appearance Deficit Disorder.

Having a dirty mind makes ordinary conversations much more interesting.

The ugliness of an airport security guard is proportionate to how intimately they want to search you.

Fashion is something that goes in one year and out the other.

Lipton have now put Viagra in their tea so that biscuits do not go limp when dunked.

Just because men have one, doesn't mean they have to be one.

Women are the only hunters who use themselves for bait.

Can a woman who absentmindedly answers the door in her nightie be described as negligent?

In a truly logical world, men rather than women would ride side-saddle.

If you don't believe men are frightened of women, go use one of those decorative towels in the bathroom. I dare you.

Sex is a part of nature, and I go along with nature. (Marilyn Monroe)

Her cup size can determine how long the hug will last.

Looking for an online date? Ask them to send a picture posing with a copy of today's newspaper.

Dear Santa, how much for your list with all the naughty girls on it?

I'm sure that ninety percent her "beauty" could be removed with a Kleenex.

Strapless gowns are a compromise between the law of decency and the law of gravity.

"Boob" is the perfect word. The B looks like an aerial view of them, the two o's look like a front view, and the b looks like the side view.

Ménage à trois - French for disappointing two girls at the same time.

Anyone who says he can see through women is missing a lot. (Groucho Marx)

Nipples are nature's thermometer.

There is a good deal to be said for blushing, but only if one can do it at the proper moment. (Mae West)

"Curb-side pickup" meant something different when I was growing up.

It's not true that I had nothing on. I had the radio on. (Marilyn Monroe)

An unmade bed is easier to get into.

Seeing how some people wear their masks during lockdown I understand why contraceptives fail.

He sent his photograph to the Lonely Hearts Club and they sent it back saying they weren't that lonely.

Watching the London Marathon and saw one runner dressed as a chicken, and another runner dressed as an egg. I thought: "This could be interesting."

Call me old fashioned, but I prefer women with eyebrows made out of hair.

It doesn't take much to make a woman happy, but it takes even less to make her mad.

She murmured to herself ruefully, "For someone who hates the circus, I sure have dated a lot of clowns."

Ironically, it's really hard when you suffer from impotency.

So I met this prostitute who said she'd do anything for $10. Guess who got his car washed?

I have an idea that the phrase "weaker sex" was coined by some woman to disarm the man she was preparing to overwhelm. (Ogden Nash)

Vasectomy: that's fair as it makes more sense to take the bullets out of the gun than to wear a bulletproof vest.

Wise not to get into a relationship until after February 14th.

Ah, the warm feeling when you see your ex has gotten fat.

If you say someone has a dirty mind, how did you know what they meant?

Ladies Only

Dear Santa, I've been good all year! OK, most of the time. I mean, once in a while. OK, bugger it, I'll buy my own stuff.

If a woman hasn't met the right man by the time she's twenty-four, she may be lucky. (Deborah Kerr)

The only thing men are good for, they're not good at.

There are only two temperatures in the office - "Satan's Armpit" or "My nipples should be registered weapons".

A man's got to do what a man's got to do. A woman must do what he can't.

Men occasionally stumble over the truth, but most of them pick themselves up and hurry off as if nothing ever happened.

The most dangerous animal in the world is a smiling woman sitting in silence.

"Interesting" is the word a man uses to describe a woman who lets him do all the talking.

Women spend more time thinking about what men are thinking than men spend thinking.

A woman wants one man to satisfy her every need. A man wants every woman to satisfy his one need.

A woman participating in a survey was asked how she felt about condoms. She said, "Depends on what's in it for me."

A woman does not spend all her time buying things; she spends part of it taking them back.

Don't piss me off. Remember, I'm a woman and have been washing blood stains from my clothes for years.

If you're sad, add more lipstick and attack. (Coco Chanel)

High heels are a man's invention to make it harder for a woman to run away.

The difference between beauty and charm: a beautiful woman is one I notice; a charming woman is one who notices me.

She admitted she would be willing to sleep her way to the top if it actually meant sleeping.

Arguing with a woman is like buying a lottery ticket, because you know you're not gonna win, but you're sure as hell going to try.

A youthful figure is what you get when you ask a woman her age.

Ladies, don't believe them. Men know exactly how much petrol is left in the tank and how far that fuel will get them.

I stopped buying women's magazines; the only time I ever see someone who looks like me is under the word "Before". (Sarah Millican)

When he wanted to take a photo of her he did not tell her to smile, he just said, "I love you," and her smile was more beautiful.

If a woman tells you her age, it's all right to look surprised, but don't scowl.

Man flu ... Woman just don't get it!

Shoe-shoppers Rule: If it feels good, it's ugly. If it looks good, it hurts.

Today's artist models are girls unsuited for their work.

Truism: hair dressers are able to create a hair style you will never be able to duplicate.

Careful, ladies, because the new iPhone X has facial recognition and some of you are going to be locked out after you wash your face off.

Always remember to speak clearly when complimenting a woman's boots. Very clearly.

Of course women don't work a hard as men, they get it right the first time.

Can you imagine a world without men? No crime and lots of happy fat women. (Nicole Hollander)

A woman saying "I'm not mad at you." is like a dentist saying "You won't feel a thing."

Intuition is that strange instinct that tells a woman she is right, whether she is or not.

During labour the pain is so great that a woman can almost imagine what a man feels like when he has a cold.

There's something incredibly beautiful about a woman that doesn't realise she's incredibly beautiful.

Marriage is just a fancy word for adopting an over grown man child who can't take care of himself.

My husband and I both have colds. I'm here in the kitchen, cleaning and he is dying!

Always felt like a man trapped in a woman's body; however, that all changed when I was born.

It is better to be looked over than overlooked. (Mae West)

Ever had a day which was a total waste of makeup?

Men and women were created equal, but women continued to improve.

I either have my hair and makeup done or I look homeless - there is no in-between.

They aren't one night stands, they're auditions.

How do you feel when you had a good hair day and no one important saw you?

If you cannot think of a way to flatter a man tell him he is the type of person who can't be flattered. Works every time.

Men go shopping to buy what they need. Women go shopping to find out what they want.

She was looking for a moisturiser that would hide the fact she'd been tired since 2010.

She rarely had time to fold laundry, but when she did, she didn't.

There are days when it takes more energy to put on the sports bra than to work out.

How come you can wear jeans everyday for weeks and nobody cares, but you wear the same shirt twice in one week and you're suddenly homeless?

Now for that natural, no makeup look ... First you'll need these eighteen cosmetic products.

The day she didn't wear any makeup four people asked her if she was OK.

The best things in life are free, but the second best things are very, very expensive.

Ninety-five percent of her arm strength came from hair-drying.

If only eyes saw souls instead of bodies, how very different ideas of beauty would be.

Whenever I don't have to wear makeup, it's a good day. (Cameron Diaz)

A wise girl knows her limits; a smart girl knows that she has none.

A jealous women does better research than ASIO.

Most wives are like ventriloquists: they stand there nodding while the dummy does all the talking.

They're called "skinny jeans", not "make you skinny jeans".

Careful when you wipe away a girl's tears that you don't remove her eyebrows as well.

Probably the worst thing you can hear when you're wearing a bikini is, "Good for you!"

A stud without a personality is like a Lamborghini without an engine.

It's great being female because:

We don't look like a frog in a blender when dancing.

We can scare male bosses with mysterious gynaecological disorder excuses.

If we forget to shave, no one has to know.

We never have to reach down every so often to make sure our private parts are still there.

We have the ability to dress ourselves.

There are times when chocolate really can solve all our problems.

We can make comments about how silly men are in their presence, because they aren't listening anyway.

Feminine intuition is a fiction and a fraud. It is nonsensical, illogical, emotional, ridiculous, and practically foolproof.

Gentlemen Only

It is true that all married men have their own way, but the trouble is they don't all have their own way of having it.

In my time, real men did not smoke cigarettes with batteries.

Women worry about the things that men forget; men worry about the things women remember.

Married men should forget their mistakes - no use two people remembering the same thing.

These old men sitting on the benches in the mall waiting on their wives to finish shopping ... Were they old when they sat down?

A man's idea of helping with the housework is lifting his legs so you can vacuum.

It's not because she didn't hear you, she's giving you a chance to change what you said.

If you want to sacrifice the admiration of many men for the criticism of one, get married. (Katharine Hepburn)

Of course men can multitask; they read on the toilet.

All men see in only sixteen colours, like Windows default settings. Peach, for example, is a fruit, not a colour. Pumpkin is also a fruit. We have no idea what mauve is.

A urinal is the one place where all men are peers.

A eunuch is a man who has had his works cut out for him.

Catch swine flu and man flu at the same time and she'll call you a chauvinistic pig.

In almost all women's shirts, the writing is across their boobs, so it's not my fault for looking.

Never make a woman mad. She can remember stuff that hasn't happened yet.

Men will confess to treason, murder, arson, false teeth and a wig before they will own up to a lack of a sense of humour.

Daughters can spend 10% more than a man can make in any usual occupation. That’s a law of nature.

When a woman asks you to guess her age, it's like deciding whether to cut the blue, red, or green wire to diffuse a bomb.

Imagine the disappointment if a wolf knew it’s descendant would be a pug. That’s how your granddad feels when he sees your man bun.

There once was an old man of Lyme who married three wives at a time; when asked, "Why a third?" he replied, "One's absurd! and bigamy, sir, is a crime!"

A fisherman is a man who spends rainy days sitting around on the muddy banks of rivers doing nothing because his wife won’t let him do it at home.

When a man gets close to a girl wearing a leather mini skirt, his heart begins to beat faster, his throat get dry, his knees weaken and he becomes irrational - because she smells like a new car.

The mythical centaur is a man with a horse where his pants ought to be.

A man believes in heredity until his son begins to behave like a delinquent.

There are few things more satisfying than putting electrical tape over the sensors of automatic doors and watching people walk right into them.

Wrestling is a sport for men with no pants to fight for a belt.

He spent the last thirty minutes trying to even up his sideburns and he's now sporting a nice mohawk.

Men do cry, but only when assembling furniture from IKEA.

Men who consistently leave the toilet seat up secretly want women to get up to go the bathroom in the middle of the night and fall in. (Rita Rudner)

I would walk over Legos for you.

Men, how disappointed do you get every time you think you've found a parking space but it's actually filled by a small car or motorcycle?

Wish they'd test James Bond by making a bomb where the wires are all one colour.

Men, because of a tragic genetic flaw, cannot see dirt until there is enough of it to support agriculture. (Dave Barry)

The only differences between men and boys are the size of their shoes and the price of their toys.

A genius is a man who can rewrap a new shirt and not have any pins left over.

If you want to know what you'll look like in ten years, look in the mirror after you've run a marathon.

That awkward moment when you're wearing Nikes and can't do it.

FEARLESS FOCUS ON FOOD

The HR manager was interviewing a nervous young man for a junior position, and in line with her advanced recruitment skills training she asked some unusual questions.

"If you could have dinner with anyone living or dead, who would you choose?"

The young man thought carefully and confidently said, "Definitely the living one."

How do dieters justify a massive mid-morning blowout, having done their dieting duty by having only a teaspoon of cottage cheese and a glass of water for breakfast? (Douglas Adams)

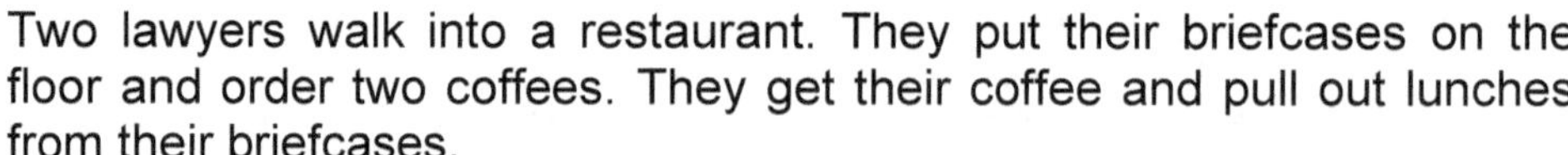

Two lawyers walk into a restaurant. They put their briefcases on the floor and order two coffees. They get their coffee and pull out lunches from their briefcases.

"Sorry," the waitress says, "you can't eat your own food here."

Solution?

The lawyers look at one another, shrug their shoulders and swap sandwiches.

A farmer is walking with a prospective buyer when they see a beautiful pig in the yard, except it has a wooden leg. The buyer asks, "Why the wooden leg?"

The farmer replies, "That pig is so smart, I let it drive the kids to school."

"Great, but why the wooden leg?"

"The pig is so smart it has a degree in horticulture and philosophy."

"Amazing! But why the bloody wooden leg?"

"Well, when you have a pig that smart you don't eat it all at once!"

They were standing in line at a fast-food restaurant, waiting to place their order. There was a big sign posted: "No bills larger than $20 will be accepted."

The woman in front of them, pointing to the sign, remarked, "Believe me, if I had a bill larger than $20, I wouldn't be eating here."

Called a local pizza place the other night and said, "Do you do takeaways?"

They said "Yes", so I said, "What's 23452 minus 345?"

Oh to be rich enough at the end of a meal to be able to throw the leftovers in the bin instead of putting them in a Tupperware container then into the fridge, only to throw them out a week later.

A waiter brings a customer the steak he ordered with his thumb over the meat.

"Are you crazy?" yelled the customer. "What are you doing with your hand on my steak?"

"What?" answers the waiter. "You want it to fall on the floor again?"

As a professional photographer, it really pisses me off when people see my work and say, "Those are nice photos. You must have a very good camera."

You wouldn't say to Gordon Ramsay: "This tarragon chicken in asparagus sorbet is delicious. You must have a superb frying pan."

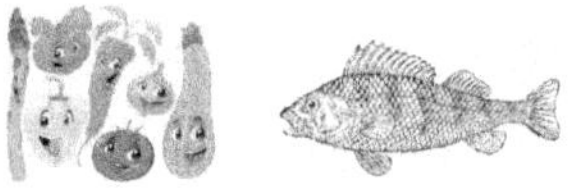

FEARLESS FOCUS ON FOOD

I'm really at my best when I grab a Tupperware container out of the cabinet and slam the door really fast so the rest don't fly out everywhere.

They say to never go shopping for food when you're hungry, but it's been a week already, and I keep getting hungrier and hungrier.

Most people don't realise this, but you can eat organic, all natural, gluten-free food without telling everyone around you.

His Nan still thinks it was a giant tiramisu that killed hundreds in Samoa. Bless her!

The trouble with eating Italian food is that five or six days later, you're hungry again.

You know you're overweight when you step on the scales and it says, "One at a time please."

It is sad when your lose a chip in the dip so you send in a rescue chip and that breaks too.

All this talk of dangerous, genetically modified food tasting horrible is nonsense. I mean, just today I had a delicious leg of salmon.

When you start eating food without labels, you no longer need to count the calories.

What do vegans get at a barbecue restaurant? Kicked out.

Nothing tops a plain pizza.

The disparity between a restaurant's price and food quality rises in direct proportion to the size of the pepper mill.

We ordered the cheeseboard to share between three people. Sort of a *fromage à trois*.

Having met some people explains why we have to do things like write "do not eat" on dry silica packets.

Tact is the art of telling someone to lose thirty pounds without ever using the word "fat".

Restaurants with peppermills the size of fire extinguishers and big red menus with the entries spelled with f's instead of s's are always expensive.

In a restaurant, the less you know about what happens in the kitchen, the more you enjoy your meal.

Never trust the food in a restaurant on top of the tallest building in town that spends a lot of time folding napkins.

Television is now evenly divided between shows about preparing food and shows about losing weight.

Wonder how many ladies starve to death each year because they cannot open jars for food.

Before vegan, vegetarian, lactose intolerant, celeriac, low carb, gluten free, Keto, Paleo, Mediterranean, Mosley, there was the Home Menu: Take it or Leave it.

That uneasy feeling that the plastic handles of overloaded supermarket plastic carry bags are getting steadily longer.

For an effective diet, just watch the food you eat. Just watch it, don't eat it.

I burned sixty calories. That should take care of the peanut I ate in 2014. (Rita Rudner)

I don't mean to brag, but I finished my fourteen-day-diet food supply in three hours and twenty minutes.

The paleo diet is to eat only foods cavemen would have eaten. So, fruity pebbles, cocoa pebbles, the oatmeal with little dinosaur eggs, etc.

A truism: people who shop in health food stores never look healthy.

The next time you feel like complaining remember your garbage disposal eats better than 30% of the people in this world.

All that is necessary for the enjoyment of sausages is confidence.

There is nothing better than a friend, unless there is a friend with chocolate.

Out of the mouths of babes comes cereal.

I'll be damned if after the five longest minutes of my life I'm going to "let cool in microwave for one minute."

How do you buy one of those plastic grocery checkout dividers when the lady behind the counter keeps putting it back?

Every few days try your jeans on just to make sure they fit. Pyjamas will have you believe all is well in the kingdom. Always.

It seems to be true that homeless people have all the shopping carts with four good wheels.

All mushrooms can be eaten, some even more than once.

The word gourmet means: "Put something weird on it, and triple the price."

He dreamed he was eating shredded wheat and woke up to find the mattress half gone.

Proven fact: diets help you gain weight more slowly and are a brief period of starvation followed by a gain of several kilos.

Pasta doesn't make you fat. How much pasta you eat makes you fat.

The odds of going to the supermarket for a loaf of bread and coming out with only a loaf of bread are three million to one.

A consumer is someone who delights advertisers by buying unnecessary products.

How many people spend more time looking in the fridge than they actually do eating?

That sound you hear when you already closed the cupboard and hear something fall ... Don't open the door - that's the sound of someone else's problem.

Please explain how a non-stick pan has a sticker stuck on it saying it's a non-stick pan.

The best diet is best described as: "unchaperoned child at a birthday party."

My current diet is similar to a nine-year-old who just found $20.

New phenomenon: people allergic to gluten free diets.

Don't you hate it when you run out of food while you're still eating?

When you hear a police car go by with sirens sounding do you ever think "they won't sell many ice-creams at that speed?"

If you think eggplant is good, you should try any other food; it's much better.

I wish all these vegetarians would stop eating my food's food.

Heartbreak is watching the waiter coming to your table with food but then take a sharp turn to a different table.

His parents were dwarves, and they struggled to put food on the table.

The inventor of the doorbell did not own a Chihuahua.

Every time I lose some weight, I find it again in the refrigerator.

Why do they call it beauty sleep when you wake up looking terrible?

Manners are the noises you don't make when eating soup.

It's a good idea to test your immune system from time to time by eating a Big Mac.

Bacon can be wrapped around everything and is essentially duct tape of food.

Food fact: everything is cold except what should be.

Want a cheap spa? Just open your dishwasher immediately it finishes its cycle.

Trouble for people living alone is it is always their turn to do the dishes.

Can someone please tell fat women that skin-tight jeans are a fashion statement not a challenge.

She maintained the only reason she was fat was because a smaller body would not be big enough to contain her personality.

Not making fun of fat people is good for their self-esteem but not good for their health.

If pubs won't serve really drunk people, why do McDonalds serve really fat people?

Nice try, fat families, with stick-figure people on the back of their van.

Vegan recipes are delicious, especially as a side dish to the meat.

Anyone who never played Tetris is probably useless at loading a dishwasher.

Ever used the "I'll let these pans soak" phrase, otherwise known as I don't feel like doing the dishes?

Who has never been caught rearranging the dirty dishes in the dishwasher after someone else had loaded it?

When a man says he'll do anything for a woman, he means slay dragons and rescue her from castle towers, not do the dishes and hang out the washing.

In Mexican restaurants everything on the menu is the same dish. The only difference is the way it's folded.

Not sure if my pants are feeling loose or the elastic has just given up the fight.

If only mosquitoes sucked fat instead of blood.

An apple a day is bullshit. Apples are dangerous. Just look at Eve, Snow White, Blackberry or any pig on a spit at a luau.

Dishes! We meet again, you dirty bastards.

A pasta-maker machine is just a Play-Doh toy for adults.

Calories (*noun*): tiny creatures that live in your wardrobe and sew your clothes a little bit tighter every night.

As soon as someone makes a time machine I'm going back to when being fat and pale was a sign of nobility.

Actually it's the fat that makes you look fat. It was never the dress.

"Put that down, you fat piece of shit" - the title of the latest dieting book.

An onion can make people cry; but sadly there's never been a vegetable that can make people laugh.

Five servings of vegetables a day. Three glasses of wine and two Bloody Mary's should cover it.

Becoming a vegetarian is a huge missed steak.

Hey, vegans, animals may have feelings, but they also have flavours.

Some days I am completely serene, but on other days trying to open the plastic bags for the vegetables in the supermarket drives me over the edge.

You are the crispy noodle in the vegetarian salad of life.

This year for Australia Day, throw veggie burgers on the BBQ and next year someone else will host it. Smart!

Vegans don't eat much; they just feed off attention.

I'm so desperately hungry I could eat a vegetable.

Got up at 5 am, went for an 8 km run, came back and prepared a vegetable smoothie ... Don't remember the rest of the dream.

Life expectancy would go ahead in leaps and bounds if vegetables smelled as good as bacon.

Stop being a vegan and start enjoying what you eat.

Every day thousands of vegetables are killed by vegetarians. Help end the violence. Eat bacon.

Expecting the world to treat you fairly because you are good is like expecting the bull not to charge because you are a vegetarian.

A fridge is just a hospice for vegetables.

Healthy eating is buying vegetables that are just going to sit at the bottom of the fridge until they go bad.

You're not a true vegan unless you tell ten people every day.

Best way to get rid of kitchen odours is to eat out.

Many people have eaten in our kitchen and gone on to lead normal, healthy lives.

If you want me to serve you breakfast in bed you'll have to sleep in the kitchen.

After the first few weeks of Weight Watchers, you're just finding your feet.

There is a pill that tricks you into thinking your body is full, but unfortunately it has 8,500 calories.

One of life's truths is: lasagne just tastes better the next day as a leftover.

Do you make lists, leave them on the kitchen table and guess what's on the list while you're in the supermarket?

Sometimes I question my sanity, but the unicorn in the kitchen said I was fine.

Nobody wants to hear about your diet; just eat your kale and be sad.

A diet is what you put off while you are putting on.

The thing I have in common with super models is that I'm hungry.

Watch the waiter's face when you ask for a diet water.

First rule of the Vegan Club. Tell everyone.

Go into the fitting room with jeans three sizes too big so you can feel what it's like to succeed at a diet.

New diet called: "I've only got $20 till Friday."

It was a brave person who first looked at a cow and said, "I think I'll just squeeze these dangly things here and drink whatever comes out." (Peter Kay)

Dieting is a game which you win when you lose.

Just switched from eating venison to pheasant. Absolute game changer.

Good etiquette means behaving yourself a little better than is absolutely essential.

Toblerone chocolate is triangular today so it fits in the box.

Because raisin muffins look like chocolate chip muffins is the reason to have trust issues.

Not sure how many chocolates equals happiness, but so far it is more than twenty-seven.

Nuts just take up space where chocolate ought to be.

The best part about Valentine's Day is the day after when all the chocolate goes on sale.

Be grateful that no matter how much chocolate you eat, your earrings will still fit.

As long as coco beans grow on trees, chocolate is fruit.

Anything is good to eat if it is made from chocolate.

Why is it that if the clothes fit, they're ugly.

I'm hungry, but I'm not "cook something" hungry.

Chemicals: noxious substances from which food is made.

Does anyone else hold the fridge door open looking for answers?

Anything with raisins in would be ten times better if they were replaced by chocolate chips. For example, in a packet of raisins.

Just did a Tupperware audit. Twelve round containers and two square lids.

Can't wait till Feb. 15th (day after Feb. 14th), otherwise known as ½-price chocolate day.

You'll never be around more people that want to kill you than when you walk into a restaurant five minutes before they close.

If you're waiting for the waiter at a restaurant, aren't you the waiter?

To avoid taking down Christmas lights, turn your house into an Italian restaurant.

An oven is a compact home incinerator used for disposing of bulky pieces of meat and poultry.

Eating a petrol station pie counts as a suicide attempt.

He'd never been swimming, and that's because it's never been more than half an hour since he last ate.

There is a restaurant called "Peace and Quiet" where kids meals cost $150.

In a restaurant, a banquet is a ten-dollar-dinner served in sufficient quantity to enable the caterer to charge fifty dollars for it.

You must eat rocket salad quickly before it goes off.

Fibre: edible wood pulp said to aid digestion and prolong life, so that we might enjoy another six or eight years in which to consume wood pulp. (Rick Bayan)

Just demolished another carton of sour cream by trying to "Push here to open".

Keep this in mind. Biscuits are a standard method for converting sugar, flour, and butter into body fat.

This salad tastes like I'd rather be fat.

Eating a salad (in public) is an overweight person's attempt to appear in control.

Every time I have a salad for lunch my stomach feels the same way a dog does when someone fake-throws a tennis ball.

Going to McDonald's for a salad is like going to a brothel for a hug.

Grocery stores could save customers a lot of time and effort by adding an "All the stuff you can microwave" aisle.

Don't trust anyone who chooses a side salad over hot chips.

If tomatoes are classed as a fruit, then tomato sauce is technically a smoothie.

A casserole is a method used by ingenious cooks to get rid of leftovers.

Most folks will agree that boiled eggs are hard to beat.

Pork chops and bacon, my two favourite animals. (Homer Simpson)

If John has one hundred pieces of bacon, and he eats twenty, what does John have? Happiness. John has happiness.

My dentist said that bacon and soda work the same as toothpaste, but he probably meant baking soda.

A pig is an animal used for converting plants into bacon.

McDonalds has a slogan: "If it's your birthday, the meal is on us." If you're in McDonalds and it's your birthday, your life sucks!

Going back to your ex is like reheating your McDonalds fries.

You can find your way across this country using McDonald stores the way a navigator uses stars.

They say that chicken and fish are the healthiest to eat, so why don't we combine them and eat penguins?

I'm so hungry I could eat something healthy.

18% of people eat because they are hungry, while 82% of people eat because it is twelve o'clock.

Showed the kids here how to eat corn-on-the-cob typewriter style, so now explaining what a typewriter is.

The only way to keep your health is to eat what you don't want, drink what you don't like, and do what you'd rather not. (Mark Twain)

Apparently you have to eat healthy more than once to get in shape. This is cruel and unfair.

Men who can eat anything they want and not gain weight should do it out of sight of the women they're married to.

Date tip: Don't ask a girl where she wants to eat. Tell her to guess where you're taking her to eat then take her to her first guess.

To lighten the pandemic, fill your mask with M & Ms and eat them like a horse.

Celery is great to eat when you're hungry and want to stay that way.

You can eat only 50% of a mermaid before you're considered a cannibal.

Ever open a bag of chips and its half full - sort of like push-up bras?

The only time to eat diet food is while you're waiting for the steak to cook.

Seize the moment. Remember all those women on the *Titanic* who waved off the dessert cart.

Most breakfast cereal is made of all those little curly wooden shavings you find in pencil sharpeners.

What makes pepperoni so good? Is it the pepper or the oni?

Let food be thy medicine and medicine be thy food. (Hippocrates)

Watermelon - it's a great fruit. You eat, you drink, you wash your face all at once.

If we shake out all of the crumbs from all of the keyboards in the world, we can end world hunger.

If you don't cut the cake into pieces and just eat the whole cake then technically you've only had one piece.

I'll just flip this omelette. OK, we're having scrambled eggs.

Calories are so damn tasty.

In a restaurant window: "Don't stand there and be hungry, come in and get fed up."

New obesity study looks for larger test group.

It's hard to lose weight when you have an overactive knife and fork.

Why is there no button on the refrigerator for locking the door from 7 pm to 7 am?

Hello customer service, I ate two happy meals and I'm still not happy.

Swiss cheese differs from camembert - better ventilation.

Indigestion happens when you love food that hates you.

A messy kitchen is a sign of happiness, as a clean kitchen is a sign of a wasted life.

The speed at which people can prepare food during a commercial break is amazing.

Surviving 21,364 days and 13 hours without using essential oils or eating kale; thank you for your prayers and support during these trying times.

Spaghetti can be eaten most successfully if you inhale it like a vacuum cleaner. (Sophia Loren)

Can anyone peel a hard boiled egg with grace?

If God wanted us to cook, why did he invent restaurants?

Anyone else try to complete a task before the microwave hits 00:00?

Discover the joy of cooking. Let your husband do it. (Julia Child)

1950's menu - eat it or starve.

Keep a potato masher in the drawer because sometimes it's fun not to be able to open that drawer.

They say every bit of chocolate you eat reduces your life by two minutes. Done the maths and it appears that I died in 1948.

The five-second rule on food is exponentially longer when no one else is around.

It is amazing how many people have such bad reactions to gluten, peanuts, and facts.

Everything tastes good when you’re on a diet.

Brunch without champagne is just a sad breakfast.

How to prepare Tofu: 1. Throw it in the trash. 2. Grill some steak.

The closest I’ve been to a diet this year is erasing food searches from my browser history.

Her dinner stomach is full, but her dessert stomach still has room.

Fish, to taste right, must swim three times - in water, in butter, and in wine.

Avoid oysters, which are clearly members of the phlegm family.

Cooking is easy, but it's not easier than not cooking.

Mayonnaise is just a moisturiser for a sandwich.

She dresses to kill and cooks the same way.

It is what's inside that matters - the fridge is a perfect example.

What did things taste like before there were chickens?

To lengthen your life, shorten your meals.

Never eat more than you can lift. (Miss Piggy)

In food, beauty comes in all shapes and sizes; small, large, circular, square, thin crust, thick crust, stuffed crust etc.

Some cannot lose weight because of metal fillings in their teeth and the fridge magnets keep pulling them into the kitchen.

During lockdown I go to my fridge many times and it cries out, "What do you want now?"

You are what you eat, so don't be fast, cheap and easy.

Enjoy long romantic walks to the fridge.

Notice to Snickers: my bite size far exceeds your pathetic estimates.

Why spend $80 on a swimsuit when you can buy 320 chicken nuggets?

Dinner time is so much better since I told the missus that the smoke alarm isn't a timer.

What some people mistake for the high cost of living is really the cost of high living.

A banana is 105 calories. A scotch is 80 calories. Choose wisely.

At the express checkout, some people count fifteen tubs of yoghurt as one item.

My superpower is picking the slowest moving queue in the supermarket.

Her cooking was so awesome even the smoke alarms cheered her on.

Warning: if you leave alphabet soup on the stove and go out, it could spell disaster.

Imagine how frustrating it would be if Tic-Tacs were individually wrapped.

DIFFERENT DRINKING DIALOGUES

A man walks into a bar and orders ten straight shots of whisky. He drinks each one down as the barman pours him the next, until the barman asks, "Are you all right? Why are you drinking so fast?".

"You'd drink fast too if you had what I've got," says the man.

"Why, what have you got?" asks the barman.

"About two dollars."

Having grown up in a small Queensland town, my friend Jim couldn't wait to tell his mum all about life in Melbourne, where he had visited.

"The malls are massive, and the restaurants are great," he said. Then he grinned. "I even went to a topless bar."

"Really?" said his mother, surprised. "What do they do if it starts to rain?"

Seeing a beautiful woman at the other end of the bar, he walks up to her and says, "Where have you been all my life?"

"Well," she says, "for the first half of it, I wasn't even born."

Me: What's the wi-fi password?

Bartender: You need to buy a drink first.

Me: OK, I'll have a beer.

Bartender: Six dollars.

Me: There you go. So what's the wi-fi password?

Bartender: "You need to buy a drink first, no spaces, all lowercase."

~

Then alcohol said, "Put that on Facebook. It will be hilarious."

But alcohol was wrong. So very wrong.

But then again, why limit Happy Hour to an hour?

~

As you well know, some of us have been known to have had brushes with the authorities on our way home from the odd social session over the years.

A couple of nights ago, I was out for a few drinks with some friends and had a few too many beers and some rather nice red wine. Knowing full well I may have been slightly over the limit, I did something I've never done before.

I took a bus home. Sure enough I passed a police roadblock, but as it was a bus they waved it past. I arrived home safely without incident, which was a real surprise, as I have never driven a bus before and am not sure where I got it!

~

A recent study found that people who drink their coffee black are more likely to exhibit psychopathic tendencies while people who order an extra hot, quad shot, non-fat, vanilla soy with extra foam, light whip with caramel drizzle coffee are most likely to be their victims.

DIFFERENT DRINKING DIALOGUES

Because alcohol tastes better than tears.

Champagne for my real friends and real pain for my sham friends. (Tom Waits)

Alcohol is a perfect solvent: it dissolves marriages, families and careers.

Lips that touch liquor touch other lips quicker.

Step aside, coffee, this is a job for alcohol.

Stop trying to make everybody happy. You are not tequila.

Nothing says "I mean business" like using a grocery cart at the bottle shop.

I've avoided abstinence for eighty-five days now.

No, sir, line dancing and a sobriety test are not the same thing.

Claustrophobia is the fear of closed spaces. For example, I am going to the liquor store and I am afraid that it is closed.

Grapes are just wine pills.

Marketing opportunity: make barstools with seat belts and dual side airbags.

Schwarzenegger isn't the only one who woke up naked next to a dumpster in 1984.

Dear liver, this month will be a rough one. Stay strong.

I like to have a martini, two at the very most. After three I'm under the table. After four I'm under my host. (Dorothy Parker)

Because he buys a great amount of alcohol he hopes he's not a shopaholic.

To the young housewife: remember that a small bottle of sherry not only will decorate the table but also will hide your cooking mistakes.

Sometime I take a bath because it's awkward drinking wine in the shower.

She didn't drink because she wanted to know when she was having a good time.

He doesn't even call it a hangover anymore - it's just morning.

There's nothing wrong with sobriety in moderation.

Your friends don't care if your house is clean; they care that you have wine.

I don't know exactly whose health I'm drinking to, but they're going to be immortal at this rate.

If you don't drink, smoke or drive a car you are a tax avoider.

People don't always drive the speed limit but they generally do when they've had a little too much to drink.

After a hard night of boozing, stepped on the scale and it showed a loss of three kilos; hence dignity weighs three kilos. Who would have thought?

He knew there was little chance that the solution to the problems would be at the bottom of that whiskey bottle, but the important thing is that he tried.

Alcohol gives you the ambition to do anything, while simultaneously taking away your ability to do so.

On being told by her doctor not to touch anything alcoholic she got a divorce.

Not an alcoholic, just got lots of things to celebrate.

Gold Lotto gives you one in two hundred million chances you won't have to work tomorrow. Alcohol gives you one in five.

In alcohol's defence, I've done some stupid stuff while I'm sober too.

Alcoholism is a disease, but it's the only disease that you can get yelled at for having. (Mitch Hedberg)

Alcohol is one of the quickest vehicles with which we escape shyness, our problems, and self-consciousness - for a few hours.

Millions of deaths would not have happened if it weren't for the consumption of alcohol. The same can be said about millions of births.

The label says: "Alcohol may intensify the effects of this medication." So is this a warning or a suggestion?

It turns out my high school chemistry teacher was right. Alcohol *is* a solution.

Can't we arrange another day between Saturday and Sunday?

The time you enjoyed wasting is not time wasted.

A smart man only believes half of what he hears; a wise man knows which half.

He drinks with impunity or anyone who invites him.

If you drink enough, your brain starts photoshopping people.

I'm giving up drinking for a month. Sorry, punctuation ... I'm giving up. Drinking for a month.

Sometimes I drink water - just to surprise my liver.

Women won't even brag about giving birth, but we men, when we fix a doorknob, drinks are on the house!

Yoga class? I thought you said pour a glass.

"Will I be able to drink with these?" is usually the first question when receiving a new prescription from the doctor.

If they don't want you to drink and drive, why put big car parks at pubs?

He only drinks a little, but when he does he turns into another person and that person drinks a lot.

Being sober delivers almost everything drinking promised.

When his doctor asked him if he drank to excess, he told him he would drink to anything.

Buy your mother a case of the very best wine because you are the reason she drinks.

Who's this "moderation" people keep telling me to drink with?

The most expensive thing about having children is the amount of wine you have to drink.

Wine is to women as duct tape is to men - it fixes everything.

Ten percent of road accidents are due to drunken driving. Which means, it is a logical statement that 90% of accidents are due to driving without drinking!

She's not a social drinker - it's mostly work related.

Oops, my "check liver" light just came on.

Drink green beer on St Patricks Day. It counts as a vegetable.

He was sober for more than two hundred days. Not in a row, you understand, but in general.

Just spilled whiskey all over my insides.

The difference between a dog and a fox is about five drinks.

It is a little known fact that drinking too much vodka can cause you to develop a Russian accent.

There will come a day when your kids will be old enough so that you can drink with them and not because of them.

Have fun with the waiter. When they ask you to try the wine at the table, sniff it, swirl it, sip it and say, "Yes, that should get me pissed."

Never drink water; it will become habit-forming. (WC Fields)

A temperance adherent is the sort of person one wouldn't care to drink with, even if they drank.

Coaster? You're assuming I plan to put my drink down?

Eating too much, drinking too much, impulse buying, and driving too fast are not indications of stress, they are my idea of a perfect day.

If we start calling it "potato juice", vodka becomes a health drink.

Amazing the things you say you'll never do again when your head is lying next to a toilet.

The beauty of vodka is that it looks like water, while the beauty of the workplace is that water bottles are allowed.

Vodka is just potatoes that made the right career choices.

Vodka is not the answer but it's worth a shot.

Keep an identical glass of vodka next to the water on your bedside table for a refreshing morning game of Russian Roulette.

Roses are red, violets are blue, vodka costs less than dinner for two.

Good morning, quarantine mates. How much vodka goes into scrambled eggs?

Potatoes make chips, French fries, crisps and vodka. It's like the other vegetables are not even trying.

Vodka mixes well with everything except decisions.

Our town is so small we don't have a town drunk so we take turns.

Be careful: drunken words are often sober thoughts.

There can be nothing more frequent than an occasional drink. (Oscar Wilde)

Life is not a fairy tale, and if you lose your shoe at midnight you're probably drunk.

Put candles in a cake, it's a birthday cake, but put candles in a pie, and somebody's drunk in the kitchen.

You've never been truly drunk until you've had to use a barstool as a walker to get home.

The word "Karaoke" is Japanese for "Drunk with Microphone".

I can always tell when I'm drunk 'cos I tend to drop things ... like my standards.

Drunk's Postulate: just because you can't dance doesn't mean you shouldn't dance.

He is not drunk, who from the floor, can rise and stand and shout for more. (Ogden Nash)

If you are naturally opposed to water in its undiluted state, dilute it with a little scotch.

BEER

Beer makes you feel the way you ought to feel without beer. (Henry Lawson)

Poured beer over my garden before planting the lawn. I hoped the grass would come up half cut.

Roses are red, beer is great, poems are hard.

Water is the most essential element in life because without it you cannot make beer.

Why do beer companies bother with an expiration date when it's never going to make it anywhere near that?

No, a balanced diet is not a beer in each hand.

All men hear is blah, blah, blah, blah, SEX, blah, blah, blah, FOOD, blah, blah, blah, BEER.

In dog beers I've only had one.

An eighty-one-year-old man has died on a domestic flight shortly after asking how much for a beer and a toasted sandwich.

The way dogs get excited when you throw a tennis ball is the way I feel about my first beer after work.

Never ask the policeman to hold your beer while you dig out your driver's licence.

No, a seven course meal is not a cheese burger and a six pack of beer.

Two beer or not two beer, that's the question. (William Shakesbeer)

Just bought beer on a credit card, using a fake ID, while wearing my nametag from work. All three have different names on them. God I love my boobs.

Over-priced luxury resort is one where a waiter expects a $2 tip when he presents a $9 bill for serving you a $3.50 bottle of beer.

Your kidney is a complex organ used to convert beer into urine.

Beer with zero alcohol - what a waste; that is like a nun with a D-cup.

Not one man in a beer commercial has a beer belly. (Rita Rudner)

Why does a fridge have a drawing or an imprint of a carrot on the beer drawer?

Non-alcoholic beer is like a porn movie on the radio.

WINE

Drink wine because doctors say you shouldn't keep things bottled up.

Unlike milk, it's OK to cry over spilt wine.

After the London plague they celebrated with wine and orgies. Do you know if anything similar has been arranged for the end of Covid?

There is truth in wine and children. (Plato)

Meals served without wine are rarely worth eating.

We have too much wine, said no one ever.

There should be an app which, instead of telling you how many calories you've burned, should tell you how many wines you've earned.

Who is the genius who decided to call it Cask Wine and not Cardboardeaux?

She enjoyed a glass of wine each night for the health benefits. The other glasses she enjoyed were for her witty comebacks and flawless dance moves.

He'd never owned a winery but was pretty sure he had drunk one.

They should put more in a wine bottle so there is enough for two people.

During Covid the best way to avoid touching your face is to have a glass of wine in each hand.

She has one glass of red wine a day for her health - the rest of the bottle is because she likes being drunk.

A mother's sacrifice is not giving birth, it's going nine months without wine.

Wine tasting is very disappointing. I prefer wine consuming where the server gives you a bottle and leaves you alone. I don't need a history of how these grapes were stomped, and I'd appreciate more than a thimble-sized cup.

Diet tip: if you think you're hungry, you might actually just be thirsty, so have a bottle of wine first and then see how you feel.

They should have put this wine back in the cat.

There is no longer a need for am and pm, just coffee time and wine time.

There are fifteen muscles activated when opening a bottle of wine. See, fitness is my passion.

Online shopping because it is frowned upon to be in a store with no bra, sweat pants and a glass of wine.

Make wine out of raisins so you don't have to wait for it to age. (Steven Wright)

Never mind the cut finger or the black eye, the important thing is that the wine bottle is open.

The answer may not lie in the bottom of a wine bottle, but you should always check.

COFFEE 

Good thing Noah took those two coffee beans on board.

Decaffeinated coffee is useless brown water.

Before coffee in the morning I hate everybody. After coffee I feel good about hating everybody.

She was always smiling from the way he made her feel. He was hot, dark and steamy and gave her life meaning. He was coffee.

Decaffeinated coffee is like a hooker who only wants to cuddle.

Most days I do not rise and shine. I just caffeinate and hope for the best.

Poured Red Bull into my coffee this morning and now I can see sounds.

Coffee is starter fluid for the morning impaired.

My morning coffee makes me feel like I have it all together. I don't, but it feels like it.

After eleven cups of coffee you cannot even blink any more.

Morning coffee; Mother Nature's jumper cables.

If you love a friend let them go. If they return with coffee it was meant to be.

Dinosaurs never had coffee and we saw how that turned out.

Coffee in England always tastes like a chemistry experiment. (Agatha Christie)

The coffee was so strong it snarled as it lurched out of the pot.

Do you know how helpless you feel if you have a full cup of coffee in your hand and you start to sneeze? (Jean Kerr)

Coffee spelled backwards is "eeffoc". You need to know that I don't give eeffoc until I've had my morning coffee.

Coffee on Sunday is recreational, but on weekdays it is medicinal.

Death before decaf!

Coffee is a liquid hug to your brain.

If this is coffee, please bring me some tea; but if this is tea, please bring me some coffee. (Abraham Lincoln)

Self-test for coffee addiction:

You haven't blinked since the last lunar eclipse.
Your eyes stay open when you sneeze.
Your T-shirt says, "Decaffeinated coffee is the devil's blend."
You go to AA meetings just for the free coffee.
Instant coffee takes too long.
You can thread a sewing machine, while it's running.

ENTERTAINMENT

People are sheep. TV is the shepherd.

In Hollywood, if you don't have a shrink, people think you're crazy.

Why does ballet have a 't' at the end?

Dancing, like robbery, requires split-second timing.

Ballet is like dreaming on your feet.

Hollywood is where they shoot too many pictures and not enough actors.

My neighbours were listening to some pretty cool music until the bastards asked me to turn it down.

Dancing is the vertical expression of a horizontal desire legalised by music. (George Bernard Shaw)

Dancing is the art of getting your feet out of the way faster than your partner can step on them.

Party trick: remove your dentures periodically to frighten your grandchildren or provide accompaniment to Spanish music.

Part of the joy of dancing is conversation. Trouble is men can't talk and dance at the same time.

I'm a method actor. I spent years training for the drinking and carousing I had to do in this film. (George Clooney)

You'd be surprised how much it costs to look this cheap. (Dolly Parton)

Don't look at your feet to see if you are doing it right. Just dance.

People who dance are considered insane by those who cannot hear the music.

The last time I danced like nobody was watching, someone stabbed me with an EpiPen.

Dance like no one is watching because they are not. They're looking at their phones.

Dance like no one's going to put it on YouTube.

That's what show business is, sincere insincerity.

To get into show business, hard work, perseverance, and discipline: all the things you need particularly when you have no talent. (Dean Martin)

Boxing is just show business with blood.

Television is an invention that permits you to be entertained in your living room by people you wouldn't have in your home.

Television is a weapon of mass distraction.

Have you noticed that families on television never watch television?

Remote controls let you see that there's nothing worth watching on TV a lot faster.

On television and in the movies ever wondered why ...

- aliens are always immune to bullets.
- all cars will explode when wrecked.
- court cases are all solved with a surprise witness.
- explosions in space make noise.
- good guys always shoot better than bad guys.
- good guys can get two hundred shots out of a six-shooter.
- haunted houses are never locked.
- if there's a thunderstorm, someone will be murdered.
- martial artists never get killed by bullets.
- no one does housework, but all homes are clean.
- only thin beautiful woman ever need to be rescued.

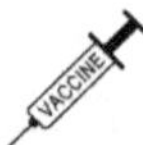

HERE'S TO YOUR HEALTH

A TEACHABLE MOMENT

Imagine a person who has a weight problem and a heavy smoking habit, to which he will not face up. Let's assume that for his height and build, he carries far too many kilos and smokes forty a day. His doctor has warned him about it, his friends have ribbed him on the subject. His wife, at careful moments, has tried to raise the subject to no avail. Almost daily, through the television ads, he is reminded of the risks he is subjecting himself to and all to no effect.

One day at work, he suffers terrible, sharp, stabbing pains in the chest and tingling in his arm and fingers. He is forced to fight desperately for breath as his pulse races out of control. He slumps across the desk, pale, afraid, weak ... vulnerable.

His doctor, seated in a nearby chair, speaks directly and sombrely about the need for weight control and stopping smoking. This time our friend hears and heeds. *Life has brought to him a "teachable moment".*

In the surgery of a very expensive private dentist the patient asks, "How much do you charge for a tooth extraction?"

"Four hundred dollars, sir."

"Four hundred dollars for two minutes work. That's outrageous!"

"If sir would prefer, I can remove it very slowly."

She went to the hospital because her whole body hurt. She told the doctor that wherever she touched herself it would hurt. The doctor told her to demonstrate. She touched her nose and it hurt. She touched her stomach and it hurt. She touched her foot and it hurt.

The doctor made the correct diagnosis that her finger was broken.

He went to the hospital to visit his mother-in-law, who was in a serious condition. On the way back his very worried wife asks, "So, honey, how's my mum doing?"

He replies, "She looks great! She is in good health. She will still live for many years. Next week she will be released from the hospital and will come and live with us forever!"

"Wow that's amazing!", says the wife. "But this is very strange. Yesterday she seemed to be on her deathbed, the doctors said she had only a few days to live."

"Well, I don't know how she was yesterday.", he replied, "But today when I arrived at the hospital, the doctor told me that we should prepare for the worst."

One of the questions asked in the entrance exam for medical school was to rearrange the letters PNEIS into the name of an important human body part which is most useful when erect. As it turned out the word was "spine".

Exercise tip: if you put your Fitbit in the dryer, you can get a head start on your steps by getting 3,800 steps in even before you put on your pants.

The secret of health for both mind and body is not to mourn for the past, nor to worry about the future, but to live the present moment wisely and earnestly. (Buddha)

Back in my day Vaping was called Vicks VapoRub.

HERE'S TO YOUR HEALTH

It's a universal lie that the doctor will be with you in a couple of minutes.

Looking at this email from my doctor. Where did he even get that font you cannot read?

Just because your doctor has a name for your condition doesn't mean he knows what it is.

Remember this: the person who came last in the medical graduating class is still called "doctor"!

Some people think doctors and nurses can put scrambled egg back in the shell.

A wise doctor once wrote ~«őʒ øѣщfŋ ʤ𝔇႘ϑ شک ѩӂӥ.

You may not be able to read your doctor's handwriting or prescription, but notice his bill is always neatly typewritten.

They certainly give strange names to diseases. (Plato)

Exercise tip: run early in the morning before your mind knows what you are up to.

I'm not feeling well. I need a doctor immediately. Ring the nearest golf course.

You do realise that the doctor hopes you fall ill don't you?

With COVID we can have gatherings of eight people without any issues. I don't know eight people without issues.

Is it possible to mistake schizophrenia for telepathy? I hear you ask.

Before COVID we used to eat cake that someone had blown out all the candles on it.

It is clear that companies that make medicine have no idea what fruit tastes like.

People who say laughter is the best medicine have never tried morphine.

Why do I have to take medication to stop me from slapping people who should be on medication?

A baby was born laughing really hard with its fists closed, and the confused doctor unfolded its tiny fingers to find a birth control pill.

Why are doctors so afraid of apples anyway?

Beware of the physician who is great at getting out of trouble.

Ask your doctor who his doctor is then switch doctors.

When the dentist asks me when was the last time I flossed, I remind him he should know; he was there.

Fat men are good natured because they can neither fight nor run.

Been to the dentist several times so I know the drill.

Don't sweat the small stuff, and it's all small stuff.

If you want a committed man, look in a mental hospital.

Loving your body only when it is in perfect shape is like loving your kids only when they are well behaved.

If you can't sleep, count sheep. Don't count endangered animals. You will run out.

Heart palpitations count as cardio, right?

Oh yeah, and where was the Benadryl and sterilisation kit and EpiPen when I got that bee sting as a kid? I could have been killed!

Diagnosis is a physician's forecast of the disease by the patient's pulse and purse. (Ambrose Bierce)

Every single person frozen to death on Mt Everest was once a highly motivated person. Stay lazy, my friends.

She was in therapy to learn how to deal with people who should be in therapy.

Medical fact. Swearing profoundly, loudly and long after hitting oneself can reduce the pain by up to 50%.

An ambulance is a vehicle used to show lawyers where the accident is.

Doctor said she thought it possibly was curvature of the spine but that was just a hunch.

The doctor told me to avoid unnecessary stress, so I didn't open his bill.

There is nothing more laughable than a doctor who does not die of old age.

I haven't eaten an apple in a week and the doctors are slowly getting through the barricade. I won't last very long. Tell my family I love them.

Specialists are doctors whose patients are expected to confine their ailments to office hours.

Doctors write the prescriptions illegibly so you can't see that it says: "This one has medical insurance. Don't kill him."

Pilates? Heavens no. Thought you said pie and lattes.

Oft-forgotten fact: even paranoids have enemies.

My doctor told me to have fewer dinners for four unless there are three other people present.

Get well cards are becoming so humorous that if you don't get sick you are missing half the fun. (Flip Wilson)

I'm sick of saying during Covid, "I forgot my mask," like I'm Batman or something.

Thought about losing weight once but hate losing so didn't.

There's that new virus going around called Unused Sick Days - apparently it's very contagious.

Allergies are nature's way of saying, "I know you're not sick, but I want you to feel like you are anyway!"

Bandaids come in two varieties - the kind that won't stay on and the kind that won't come off.

It is not uncommon to be in two minds whether to believe a diagnosis of schizophrenia.

Roses are red, violets are blue,

I've got Alzheimer's, cheese on toast.

There probably was a time when the idea of having a toilet inside a house was repulsive. (Mokokoma Mokhonoana)

Do not get your flu shot at work because one day you might want a sickie using having the flu as the excuse.

To accommodate you anti-vaxers we have provided a window next door where you can stare at your own reflection since apparently you are the only person you care about.

She bought her husband a "Get Better" card. He wasn't sick, she just wanted him to be better.

The advantage of exercising every day is that you die healthier.

If you want to know the correct way to perform an exercise, the answer is: "Whatever hurts most."

I exercised and ate healthy today so I'd better bloody wake up skinny tomorrow.

If you think a minute goes really fast you've never been on a treadmill.

Exercise is poor people's plastic surgery.

My idea of exercise is a brisk sit. (Phyllis Diller)

Aerobics is a series of exercises which helps convert fats, sugars, starches into aches, pains and cramps.

Exercise is vulgar - it makes people smell.

Surprised at how winded I was by this exercise then found out this was just the orientation tour of the gym.

Ever noticed exercise and extra fries sound so similar?

Exercise would be more fun if calories screamed while you burned them.

I signed up for an exercise class and was told to wear loose-fitting clothes. If I had any I wouldn't have signed up in the first place.

If it weren't for the fact that the TV set and the refrigerator are so far apart, some of us wouldn't get any exercise at all.

A sure cure for seasickness is to sit under a tree. (Spike Milligan)

Careful: if you exercise, your skin will flush, your heart races, you get sweaty and short of breath. Very dangerous.

I can't exercise for long periods. When I get back from a run my wife usually asks if I've forgotten something.

Exercise is a celebration of what your body can do, not punishment for what you ate.

Many people are so lazy, they don't even exercise good judgement.

With gym fee $120 a year, that's a bit steep for $60 a visit.

Atrophy: an award given to those who do not exercise.

Exercise can add years to your life. For example, I just ran two kilometres and I now feel like I'm eighty-two.

He exercises by running up the street knocking on all the doors - Jehovah's Fitness.

Entered what I ate today into my new fitness app and it just sent an ambulance to my house.

A lack of exercise is now causing as many deaths in the developed world as smoking, a study suggests. So I've started jogging to the tobacconist's every morning.

Many people would go to the gym more often if it had a smoking section.

Every time she heard the dirty word "exercise" she would wash her mouth out with chocolate.

Easy exercise is to spend time at the gym doing diddly squats.

Need exercise? Yoga class is great, because you can close your eyes and imagine yourself in a relaxing place, like on your couch not doing yoga.

You know that you're out of shape when you can't pull supermarket shopping trolleys apart.

Optometrist's slogan: "Buy your glasses here if you ever want to see your children again."

He's in two minds whether to believe his diagnosis of schizophrenia.

Those with arthritis agree it is just twinges in the hinges.

Serotonin and dopamine. Technically the only two things you enjoy.

The producers of cherry-flavoured cough syrup obviously have never tasted a cherry before.

Psychology can be defined as the science that tells you what you already know in words you can't understand.

I never thought I would be one of those people who get up early to hit the gym every day. I was right.

So out of shape I can't even jog my memory without breaking into a sweat.

Jogging is for people who aren't intelligent enough to watch television.

The trouble with jogging is that, by the time you realise you're not in shape for it, it's too far to walk back.

Hearty laughter is a good way to jog internally without having to go outdoors.

Nothing makes a smoker happier than to see an old person smoking.

There is no cure for birth and death, so just enjoy the interval.

When he was dying he wanted his last words to be, "I left three million dollars under the ..."

Instead of red-eye reduction on camera's why can't they make one with double-chin reduction?

When you see ads on TV with smiling, happy housewives using a new cleaning product, the only thing you want is the medication they must be on.

My psychiatrist and I had a major breakthrough. Now he can hear the voices too.

I went on the pill when I was sixteen and put on eighteen kilos. That proved to be an effective contraceptive. (Jo Brand)

Never seen anyone smiling while jogging, so that's all you need to know about that.

Make tomorrow's colonoscopy special by eating a full meal of glitter.

For truly effective motivation, get on a treadmill naked in front of a mirror.

Note: forty-five minutes on the treadmill is no big deal if you don't turn it on.

If you can afford a gym membership, you can afford deodorant.

Why do gyms have mirrors? You know what you look like; that's why you're here.

Her bathing suit said she should go to the gym but her trackies said, "Nah, girl, you're all good."

You won't believe this. I saw someone put a bottle of water in the Pringles chip box at the gym.

I've done a lot of stupid stuff in my life, but at least I've never signed up at the gym in January.

Unless you fell off the treadmill no one wants to hear about your workout.

The gym offered me free membership for life if I posed for a "Don't let this happen to you" poster.

People will pay to be subjected to medieval torture devices if you call the place a "gym".

Can't believe you didn't go to the gym today? That's a record - five years in a row now.

Eighty-seven percent of gym members don't even know their gym is closed during Covid.

Would people still go to the gym if Instagram didn't exist?

Why join a gym if you have Photoshop?

Bad news for agoraphobics: a cure is just around the corner.

It is not possible to praise nurses too highly.

The great thing about homeopathy is that you can't overdose on it; but then you might drown.

That .01% of germs that can't be killed by hand sanitizer must be really, really bad.

Hand sanitizer. Helping you find cuts you never knew you had.

My body has absorbed so much soap, sanitizer and disinfectant, when I pee it cleans the toilet.

When the hospital makes you put on one of those little gowns, you know the end is in sight.

A hospital bed is a parked taxi with the meter running.

It's hard to feel fit as a fiddle when you're shaped like a cello.

If losing weight is not working for you, concentrate on getting taller.

Hospitals are places where friends of the patient go to talk to other friends of the patient.

Life has its ups and downs. We call them squats.

It's the holiday season, so set your bathroom scales back five kilos.

Refuse to spend your life worrying about what you eat. There is no pleasure worth forgoing just for an extra three years in the geriatric ward.

What linguistic genius set up sneeze and wheeze to rhyme so very perfectly with allergies?

Note that the first four letters in health are "heal".

Three out of five people go to psychiatrists; the other two are psychiatrists

The government is to allow greater Medicare rebate on vasectomies - it wants to encourage more cuts to the private sector.

Nicotine anonymous. When you feel the craving for a smoke, you ring another member, they come over and you get pissed together.

For some fun, go to the pharmacy, buy a box of condoms and ask where the fitting room is.

First need in the reform of hospital management? That's easy! The death of all dieticians, and the resurrection of a French chef.

Doctors are always working to preserve our health and cooks to destroy it, but the latter are the more often successful. (Denis Diderot)

Half the modern drugs could well be thrown out the window, except that the birds might eat them.

Just because you're not sick doesn't mean you're healthy.

We should be made to understand that we must take charge of our own life. Don't take your body to the doctor as if he were a repair shop.

Many people treat their bodies as if they were a rental car - something they are using to get around in but nothing they genuinely care about understanding.

Health is not simply the absence of sickness.

Jogging tip: start slow and taper off.

If God invented marathons to keep people from doing anything more stupid, the triathlon must have taken him completely by surprise.

Runner's logic: I'm tired. I'll go for a run.

Happiness is nothing more than good health and a bad memory.

Homes should be clean enough to be healthy and dirty enough to be happy.

He just lost five kilos on a new diet called "the flu".

Exercise: the joy of flex.

He's trying to lose just enough weight so that his gut doesn't jiggle when he brushes his teeth.

That prince in Sleeping Beauty doesn't get enough credit for kissing someone who hadn't brushed her teeth in forever.

Drugs may lead to nowhere, but at least it's the scenic route. (Steven Wright)

We need a prescription drug that gets rid of the side effects of all the other prescription drugs.

Ever wonder why exhaustion is sufficient cause for the hospitalisation of a celebrity yet is the normal state of existence for the rest of the working world?

You mean to tell me people run? On purpose? When nobody is chasing them?

Sneezing is a really good way of working out exactly how full your bladder is.

The location of your mailbox shows you how far away from your house you can go in a robe before you start looking like a mental patient.

She could turn more heads than a chiropractor.

If you don't know what introspection is you need to take a long, hard look at yourself.

The best medicine for rheumatism is to thank the Lord it isn't gout or shingles.

Nine out of ten dermatologists agree that towels are the leading cause of dry skin.

A male gynaecologist is like an auto mechanic who never owned a car.

I smoke in moderation, only one cigar at a time. (Mark Twain)

Not suggesting he is a hypochondriac but the only thing he hasn't contracted yet is a computer virus.

Not smoking is not an achievement. Like virginity, it comes standard.

Being a hypochondriac is going to save my life one day.

The problem is not that obesity runs in the family; rather the problem is that nobody runs in the family.

Minor surgery is an operation performed on somebody else.

If the bathroom isn't flooded did the kids even brush their teeth?

Instead of calling them New Year's Resolutions, I prefer Casual Promises to Myself That I am Under No Obligation to Fulfil.

With a dentist's appointment tomorrow you have nineteen hours to do six months of flossing.

Fresh air impoverishes the doctor. (Danish Proverb)

Can they make bandaids that are easier and faster to unpack so I don't bleed to death?

Which is the non-smoking lifeboat?

I told my psychiatrist that I've been hearing voices. He told me that I don't have a psychiatrist.

Then there was the suicidal homeopath who took 1/50th of the recommended dose.

Self-checkout was invented by a guy who had to buy female hygiene products.

Anyone else like to be a "Retired Lottery Winner" when they grow up?

So what's it like to have voices in your head? I hear you ask.

According to obituary notices, a mean and useless citizen never dies. (Clarence Darrow)

Start wearing nicotine patches as a way of easing yourself into a smoking habit.

The only A+ I ever got in life is my blood type.

There's someone for everyone, and the one for you is a psychiatrist.

Saw a guy with a *Support Dyslexia* bumper sticker on the *front* of his car.

Say no to drugs, but if you're talking to drugs, it's too late.

The psychic was hopeless - she didn't even know I was going to run out without paying.

I've forgotten more than most people know about amnesia.

In the mini-bus, the weakest bladder determines pit stops, not the strongest.

My friend told me he had the body of a Greek god. I had to explain to him that Buddha is not Greek.

I'm starting to lose my mind, but as long as I have the part which tells me when I have to pee I should be OK.

Since it's the thought that counts I'll keep thinking about exercising.

There's nothing wrong with him that a vasectomy of the vocal cords wouldn't fix.

Conjunctivitis.com - there's a site for sore eyes. (Tim Vine)

My son screamed like a little girl when he saw a spider, so no paternity test was needed.

Psychiatry enables us to correct our faults by confessing our parents' shortcomings.

Tombstone read: "Died because I did not send that email to ten people."

Tombstone read: "Damn it's dark down here."

Tombstone read: "I knew this was going to happen, but not so soon."

Tombstone read: "Don't just stand there, water my flowers."

Put a "COVID QUARANTINE" sticker on the front door and you won't have problems with salesmen, thieves, or neighbours.

Remember COVID?

Never in a million years could I have imagined I would go up to a bank teller wearing a mask and asking for money.

People have sanitised clean hands but there is a ban on shaking hands.

I never thought the comment, "I wouldn't touch him/her with a six-foot pole" would become a national policy, but here we are!

This virus has done what no woman has been able to do. Cancel sports, shut down all bars and keep men at home.

2019: Stay away from negative people. 2020: Stay away from positive people.

Some needed to practise social distancing from the refrigerator.

Some people shouldn't be informed when this quarantine is over.

This Covid social distancing is a pickpocket's nightmare.

Remember when you would sneeze and someone would politely say, "Bless you."? Now they run the other way.

Relax. No matter how much weight you gained during Covid, your jewellery will still fit.

Social-distancing rules can be enhanced by eating three bulbs of garlic.

FLY ME TO THE MOON
(By Plane, Train or Automobile)

Introduction announcement by a flight attendant ...

Ladies and gentlemen, welcome aboard our tin can full of kerosene. If at any time you wish to leave this aircraft during the flight you will not be allowed back on board.

For those of you who have not been in a car since 1956, these straps are called seat belts and are to be worn when invited to.

Here we like to keep up with all the latest fashion trends, so if this flight becomes a cruise you each get your own itsy bitsy teeny weeny yellow polka-dot bikini as a flotation device.

This is fitted with a light and I have no idea how that works. If by chance it does not inflate, grab hold of your neighbour and hang on for dear life. The life jacket for your child is under the seat, so choose your child who has shown the most potential and fit it to them.

Most of you will know more than twenty-three ways to make love, but I'm here to tell you there are only six ways out of this aeroplane.

If needed, oxygen masks will drop from overhead. Once you stop screaming, place the mask over your mouth and nose. Only those of you who paid the extra $49.99 will have access to any oxygen.

Adjust your own mask first before assisting your favourite child, another passenger or your husband, who is definitely screaming louder than you are.

For those of you who did not give me your full attention, good luck!

"Ladies and gentlemen, please remain in your seats until the trainee captain and his magnificent crew have brought the aircraft to a screeching halt against the gate. And, once the tire smoke has cleared and the warning bells are silenced, we will open the door and you can pick your way through the wreckage to the terminal".

When waiting to collect your luggage from the airport conveyor belt you'll notice that on the next conveyor belt adjacent there is a solitary bag going around and around and around uncollected.

This has been placed there by the baggage handling staff to take your mind off the fact that your bags will be shortly landing in Vladivostok. (Douglas Adams)

I was driving when I first saw the flash of a traffic camera. I figured that my picture had been taken for speeding, even though I knew I wasn't.

Just to be sure, I went around the block and passed the same spot, driving even more slowly. But again the camera flashed.

Thinking this was pretty funny, I drove past even slower three more times, laughing as the camera snapped away each time I drove by at a snail's pace.

Two weeks later, I got five tickets in the mail for driving without a seatbelt.

FLY ME TO THE MOON

Flying is the second greatest thrill known to man. Landing is the first.

A good pilot always has his mind five minutes ahead of where the aeroplane is.

The flight attendant explained that when she said to turn off all electronic devices she did not mean the husband's pacemaker.

Aeroplanes stay up in the sky in much the same way that bricks don't. (Douglas Adams)

I'm a ~~mechannick~~, ~~mecannic~~, ~~mekanic~~ ... I fix planes.

A helicopter is described as one million parts rotating rapidly around an oil leak waiting for metal fatigue to set in.

In some planes the seat in front of you comes so far back you could do dental work on the passenger there.

There ought to be a requirement that crying babies have to go into the overhead lockers.

Yes, I'm a female pilot and, as a benefit, if we get lost on the way I won't be afraid to stop and ask for directions.

The flight attendant said, "I'm sorry, sir, but I can't lift your luggage into the overhead bin. These are tits not muscles."

If something hasn't broken on your helicopter, it's about to.

Qantas, a marketing suggestion: let passengers exit the plane on the inflatable slide on their birthday.

If the wings are travelling faster than the fuselage, it's probably a helicopter and therefore unsafe.

Would passengers please refrain from smoking on this flight until you reach a designated smoking area, which, for Australia, is Sydney.

The signs on the ceiling and the disco lights on the floor will lead you to the exits.

Flying has changed so much that now a flight attendant can get a pilot pregnant.

Airlines have become so cash-strapped, they're also going to charge for emotional baggage.

Mankind has a perfect record in aviation; we never left one up there.

When a flight is proceeding incredibly well, something has been forgotten.

Airspeed, altitude, and brains. Any two are always needed to successfully complete a flight.

Weather forecasts are horoscopes with numbers.

People don't have a fear of flying, they have a fear of crashing.

How about we define a good flight by negatives: you didn't get hijacked, you didn't crash, you didn't throw up, you weren't late, you weren't nauseated by the food, you didn't have a child kicking your seat all the time. So be grateful.

Man is flying too fast for a world that is round. Soon he will catch up with himself in a great rear-end collision. (James Thurber)

To pilot requesting traffic control landing information, "The last time I gave a pilot what he wanted I was on penicillin for three weeks."

After a rough landing she asked the pilot whether they landed or were shot down.

Captain to passengers: We arrived at the terminal thirty minutes early, so to make sure we never do that again, they are going to make us sit out here for thirty minutes.

Why would you want to fly Virgin - an airline that doesn't go all the way?

I told my suitcase there will be no holiday this year. I'm now dealing with emotional baggage.

Man must rise above the Earth - to the top of the atmosphere and beyond - for only thus will he fully understand the world in which he lives. (Socrates)

There's a big difference between a pilot and an aviator. One is a technician; the other is an artist in love with flight.

The similarity between air traffic controllers and pilots is that if a pilot screws up, the pilot dies; if ATC screws up, the pilot dies.

When I fly I want the pilot to fly with their head, not their hands and feet.

There is no more exciting sport than flying, for if you lose, you die.

Ladies and gentlemen, we have on our flight today someone who is taking his first flight on his eightieth birthday. Please give a round of applause for your captain.

The optimist invents the airplane and the pessimist the parachute.

Sued the airline for the loss of baggage but lost the case.

Principles of modern law assert that you're innocent until proven guilty, yet airport security is the exact opposite of this.

TRAINS

Anyone who enjoys one liners will travel by monorail.

Ladies and gentleman, upon departing the train may I remind you to take your rubbish with you. Despite the fact that you are in something that is metal, fairly round, filthy and smells, this is a train for public transport and not a wheelie bin.

When getting a round trip ticket and asked "Where to", you should reply "Here".

Has your train of thought ever left the station without you?

The only way of catching a train I have ever discovered is to miss the train before. (GK Chesterton)

It ought to be plain how little you gain by getting excited and vexed.

You'll always be late for the previous train, and always on time for the next.

A train station is sort of a primitive airport, only you didn't have to take a cab twenty miles out of town to reach it.

Don't let your train of enthusiasm run through the station so fast that people can't get on board.

Some people spend the whole of their lives sitting waiting for one train, only to find that they never even made it to the station.

I never travel without my diary. One should always have something sensational to read in the train. (Oscar Wilde)

Trains are wonderful. To travel by train is to see nature and human beings, towns and churches and rivers, in fact, to see life. (Agatha Christie)

Waiting for inspiration is standing at the airport waiting for a train.

All train timetables are works of fiction.

AUTOMOBILES

To really freak out the salesman at a car dealership say, "Tell me if you can hear me," then get in the boot and start screaming.

The easiest way to make your old car run better is to check the prices of a new one.

The best car safety device is a rear-vision mirror with a policeman in it.

Remember you are not stuck in traffic, you *are* traffic.

The secret of safe, careful driving is to spend fifty dollars on a Chinese takeaway and put it on the passenger seat.

Cars should have a thing where, if they drive around with the indicator on for too long, they automatically pull off the road and are immobilised for ten minutes.

He who hesitates is not only lost but several miles from the next freeway exit.

It's time for a new car when you double the value of your car every time you fill the tank.

If your low-fuel light is on, putting up to $20 petrol in will not make it go out.

To upset hitchhikers, pick them up and then do a U-turn.

Pedestrians are those who thought there were a couple of litres left in the tank.

A tree never hits an automobile except in self-defence.

The speed limit here is 60 km per hour unless, of course, Mr Important is running late.

Wouldn't it be nice if the wattage of a car stereo could not exceed the IQ of the driver?

A survey has shown that the average man has had sex in a car fifteen times. Something to keep in mind next time you're looking for a used car.

The slowest drivers in the world are those who are getting out of the parking space you want to get into.

Nine out of ten foreign cars are still on the road - only one made it home.

Welcome to Western Australia. We hope you brought something to do.

Drive through the mud, they said. The mud's not that deep, they said. Bastards.

Automobile racing began five minutes after the second car was built. (Henry Ford)

When driving it is necessary to relax your muscles when you can; relaxing your brain is fatal. (Stirling Moss)

If all the cars in the Australia were placed end to end, it would probably be Easter weekend.

With each replacement of parts, a car slowly becomes Chinese.

It is not sensible to drive a truck off a cliff to test the air brakes.

The person you beat out of a prime parking space is the one you have to see for the job interview.

A parking space is an unoccupied place on the other side of the street.

The quickest way to make a red light turn green is to try to find something in the glove box. (Billy Connolly)

Stephen Hawking says we've got about one thousand years to find a new place to live, but that isn't even enough time for some people to pack.

Changed the audio of my GPS to a man's voice so now it just says, "It's around here somewhere. Keep driving for a little while."

Rules for driving in Australia:

1. Anything done while honking your horn is legal.
2. You may park anywhere if you turn your four-way indicators on.
3. A red light means the next six cars may go through the intersection.

A truly reckless driver is one who passes you when you are already exceeding the speed limit.

Car advertisements seriously overestimate how much time we spend driving around in the desert. Really?

It's really ironic that people mostly use their driver's licence to buy stuff that impairs their ability to drive.

No matter how many letters I write to the main roads department, they still refuse to start designing highways with second-chance exits.

Detour: something that lengthens your mileage, diminishes your fuel, and strengthens your vocabulary.

If you want to watch the world go by just stick to the speed limit.

It's interesting how pedestrians confuse "right-of-way" with immortality.

Beware of traffic lights which are simply a trick to get pedestrians halfway across the street safely.

Roadside sobriety test should be simply to fold a fitted sheet.

Ever think to take your kids down to the car dealership and show them the nice Aston Martin V12 Vantage you'd be driving if they had never been born?

One thing that I have never had in the glove box of my car is a pair of gloves.

Those who drive like hell are bound to get there.

Why is it that wherever I go, the world's worst drivers have followed me there?

Driving isn't even in the top five things I'm thinking about when I'm driving.

No problem texting and driving, but texting while walking downstairs, that is dangerous!

People with pierced nipples have no excuse for losing their car keys.

Going to donate some old clothes to Vinnies but first will drive around with them in the boot for three months like I usually do.

With the rise of self-driving vehicles, it's only a matter of time before we get a country song where a guy's truck leaves him too.

Driving is just like colouring in: just stay inside the lines.

Why do taxi drivers who sit down all day choose to sit on a seat made of wooden balls?

How long since you looked at your driver's licence photo to see if you can detect whether your hair is receding or not.

It is amazing how quickly the kids learn to drive a car, yet are unable to understand the lawnmower or vacuum cleaner.

Do not ever text while driving because it increases the chance of typos.

Cab drivers are living proof that practice does not make perfect.

There are the very rare few who are gifted and before GPS were able to drive and refold a road map at the same time.

Remember when petrol was so cheap you didn't shake the hose after you filled up?

People don't like it when you go the extra mile for them, especially when you are a taxi driver.

If you want to know about all the stuff wrong with your car just turn the radio down.

Ever try to remember what the small key on your key ring is for?

Remove your windscreen wipers and you won't get parking tickets.

Please don't come to my garage sale if you've ever let me borrow something.

Just backed into a parked Jaguar but left him a copy of my bank statement so he knows not to bother calling.

A garage sale is where you buy stuff from someone else's garage to store in your own.

Don't you find it odd that on *Star Trek*, when they "Boldly go where no one has gone before", they always end up meeting someone?

A Prius just tried to race me from a stop sign. I totally had it for the first 100 metres, but I can only walk so fast.

Facebook, Twitter, MySpace, WhatsApp,
Instagram, Wechat, Linkedin, Ho-Hum.zzzzzzzzzzz...

Anyone remember the good old days before Facebook, Twitter and Instagram when you had to take a photo of your dinner, then go to the chemist's shop to have it developed, wait a week, then go around all of your friends' houses to show them the picture of your dinner?

No? Neither do I.

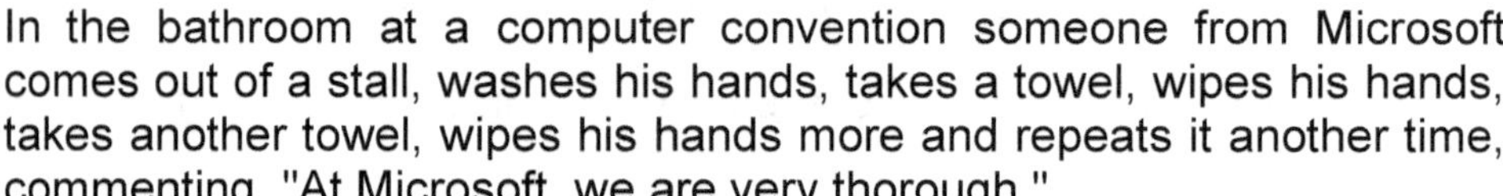

In the bathroom at a computer convention someone from Microsoft comes out of a stall, washes his hands, takes a towel, wipes his hands, takes another towel, wipes his hands more and repeats it another time, commenting, "At Microsoft, we are very thorough."

Someone from Intel comes out of a stall, washes his hands, takes a towel and wipes his hands with the single towel until the towel is all wet and his hands are dry. "We at Intel aren't just thorough, we're also efficient."

Someone from Linux comes out of a stall, walks past the sinks and comments, "We at Linux just don't piss on our hands."

If you turn the TV off today and prevent your children from using Facebook or Twitter and make them play board games like you did in 1965 you'll understand why all of your grandparents are alcoholics.

Shout-out to all those teachers who made a choice in life and are trapped in a room with twenty-five children who, when they are not on some form of social media, are vainly trying to learn to play the recorder. We salute you.

~

You #are #ridiculous #with #your #annoying #and #totally #unnecessary #use #of #hash #tags.

~

The other day during lunch break I saw one of my colleagues playing some kind of war game on his smartphone. As I poured my coffee I asked him about the game he was playing and we started small talking.

A few minutes into our small talk he stated that so far he'd spent $700 in game purchases.

I burst into loud laughter while sniggering how that was the stupidest thing and biggest waste of money I'd ever heard of!

Man, I was still laughing out loud in disbelief, walking off and even still chuckling as I entered the smoking room for a cigarette.

Facebook, Twitter, MySpace, WhatsApp, Instagram, Wechat, Linkedin, Ho-Hum.zzzzzzzzzz...

Do young people today speak English? C U I'll TXT U L8R :)

Take the door to your son's room off its hinges to update your home's privacy policy.

"The greatest thing about Facebook is that you can quote something and totally make up the source." (Julius Caesar)

To all of you who post weather maps on Facebook, you know we have the internet, right?

Computer programming is just like writing a book except if you miss a comma on page 151 the whole thing makes no sense.

If I put all of my emails on the cloud, what happens if there is a thunderstorm?

Thunder and lightning are not the gods being angry, it is Google and Microsoft fighting in the clouds.

The book, *Cloud Computing for Dummies* wasn't any help. Do you have one called *Cloud Computing for Complete Idiots*?

The angels love looking at all of your private data on the cloud.

Just printed on wireless printer but not sure which neighbour has my document.

"Username or Password Incorrect." Couldn't you just tell me which one?

Thou shalt not use the 280 characters limit as an excuse for bad grammar and/or incorrect spelling.

In these technological days it's more important to delete history than to make it.

The good news about computers is that they do what you tell them to do. The bad news about computers is that they do what you tell them to do.

Your mobile has already replaced your camera, your alarm clock, your calendar and diary, so don't let it replace your family.

Traffic lights turn green so fast, I can't even update my status.

Working in IT is like being married. When it all works well you get no thanks, but one tiny thing goes wrong and boy are you in the shit.

Don't get annoyed when your parents ask you "stupid" tech questions. They are the ones who taught you how to use the toilet, so just help them.

The most basic need on Maslow's Hierarchy of Needs is not physiological (food, shelter, warmth), it is wi-fi.

If you gets a link called "free porn" don't open it. It is a birus wich deactivates your spelchek and garblis up you riting. I also receibed it but lukily I dont does porn so I dint opin it.

The greatest fear of young people today is the message: "Low battery."

When you can download food, only then I'll be impressed with technology.

#Remembers #A #Time #When #People #Used #To #Write #Without #Using #This #?

Keep calm. Don't panic. Just turn it off and on again. See if that works.

There's life without Facebook? Really? Send me the link.

Remember when emojis were called "hieroglyphics"?

In 1980 we just got a fax at work. We didn't know we had a fax machine. The entire department just stared at it and poked it with a stick.

All our records are electronic now, so just fill out these twelve forms.

Wi-fi went down during a family dinner the other night. One kid started talking and they didn't know who he was.

You really shouldn't ignore the red squiggly lines under all of your words, but you do.

My password is the last sixteen digits of Pi, so now try to hack me, you wanker.

Cats seem to spend two thirds of their lives sleeping, and the other third making viral videos.

They are the WTF generation : Wikipedia, Twitter and Facebook.

Twitter is great if you can't afford therapy but you also don't want to get any better.

Challenge your Facebook friends to say, "The sixth sheik's sixth sheep's sick" six times quickly and then snigger quietly to yourself.

Facebook allows you to forget the birthdays of people you don't really know.

Being a little older I am grateful that every day a gentleman rings me from India and is very concerned about my computer security.

You are rarely more focused on five seconds than when you're waiting to skip an ad on the internet.

Autocorrect changed Morning Run to Morning Rum. Change of plans, friends!

What is it with people that won't embrace modern technology? Answers on a postcard please.

If car manufacturers had kept up with technology like the computer industry has, we would all be driving $25 cars that got 1000 km per litre.

Computers could be more encouraging. Instead of "invalid password", why not something like, "Ooooh, you're so close!"

The problem with cars having the internet on the dashboard is that this will distract drivers from texting.

Twitter is currently valued at $18 billion, or $1 for every hour it has wasted.

The biggest lie in the entire universe is, "I have read and agree to the Terms and Conditions."

If your kids text you "plz" which is shorter than "please", text back "no" which is shorter than "yes".

Thanks to Twitter, I can't go anywhere without my mobile. Quick question. Do I take this man to be my lawfully wedded husband?

I wonder if Bono has found what he's looking for yet? Although, if you're reading this, Bono, I'd try down the side of the couch.

You can get numerous chances to become a millionaire daily. All you have to do is open your "Spam" folder.

Twitter has saved me from a terrifying keeping-my-thoughts-to-myself addiction.

Facebook needs three buttons: Like, Dislike, Stop being stupid.

Don't text to me in that tone of voice.

Before social networking you could just completely forget someone existed and it was ... great!

If I don't log into Facebook two days in a row, call the police because someone must've kidnapped me.

Be really thankful you had a childhood before social media took over.

The only guy on the internet that I trust with my personal data is that Nigerian prince.

Look at how much Egyptians worshipped cats. Then go look at Facebook for about five minutes.

And just like that, people on Facebook went from being politicians to being epidemiologists.

Send a co-worker a fifteen-page document as fifteen one-page PDF files rather than one fifteen-page PDF file. Passive-aggressive level achieved.

English teachers on Facebook must feel the same hopelessness as dentists do when they're at a lolly shop.

People that cheat on their taxes disgust me. This is not the world I want to raise my twenty-eight dependents in.

During quarantine I'm working from home but as a bartender.

I don't mean to brag, but a lot of people have discovered how the unfollow button on Facebook works because of me.

Is it just me, or is anyone else finding it difficult to log on to dyslexics.moc?

Facebook: the only place in the world you can be social while being antisocial.

If you're ever wondering who your real friends are all you have to do is delete your Facebook account for about week without saying anything and see who calls.

The man who invented autocorrect pissed away in his sleep last night.

People who publicly announce they're "taking a break" from social media are merely disgruntled that they have only ten friends and even those ten never comment.

HP? I'd like to make a return. I ordered a Laser Jet and you sent me a printer.

When I was a kid we used to keep our Facebook account secure with a lock and key. We used to call it a diary.

The phrase "a stone's throw" has been discontinued. Please use "in wi-fi range" from now on.

The minute you post an incorrect spellling on line you find a hundred unemployed teachers on social sites.

Yes, your smart devices can talk to each other now, and they are giggling about you behind your back.

Facebook needs to make a "Slap you in the face with a dictionary" button.

Something I never said as a kid: my book stopped working.

Just blocked someone on Facebook for correcting my grammar and it feelted good.

Ever wonder how many mini walnuts you can fit in each cheek before your facial recognition stops working?

People who get offended on Facebook are the same people that take mini golf seriously.

Remember when social networking was something that happened in person? How awkward.

Don't go to high school reunions, because Facebook lets you judge your old classmates every day and not just every ten years.

Now accepting friends on Facebook that live on a lake, have a wine cellar and a boat and/or jet skis.

Maybe my parents told me how proud they were of me because they didn't have Facebook back then.

The best sign of a happy loving relationship between two people on Valentine's Day is no sign of it all on Facebook.

Want to lose an amazing social life? Sign up for Facebook.

Go to the gym on one of those one-day free passes, take 365 selfies, then post one every day on Facebook.

Facebook. Because sunlight isn't for everyone.

Can't see an end, have no control, don't think there's any escape, don't even have a home anymore - definitely time for a new keyboard.

Do some of your "friends" on Facebook need to be reminded that high school is over?

A clean house and finished projects is the sign of someone who hasn't looked at Facebook in a while.

Re Twitter: the supply of words on the world market is plentiful, but the demand is falling.

I don't have a Facebook or Twitter account so I just go around announcing out loud what I'm doing at random times. Have three followers so far, two of whom I think are police.

Do people who are fasting put pics of empty plates on Instagram?

If you're feeling bored, find a group photo of four girls on Instagram, comment "You three look great!", and then wait.

Thank you all for the birthday wishes and thank you Facebook for reminding them.

FACEBOOK is the second most popular word that starts with "F" and ends with "K".

Facebook needs a button that's the equivalent of kicking someone under the table to stop them from making a fool of themselves.

Facebook, making people who wouldn't talk in the street wish each other happy birthday since 2004.

Look, meanwhile on Facebook someone has made a casserole!

I love updating my Facebook status while crossing the stre

The strength of Twitter is that you can do anything. The weakness is that you will.

Difficult choice - a phone or a life?

Without my mobile phone I would not be able to:

1. *know what time it is.*
2. *do simple arithmetic.*
3. *know a single phone number.*
4. *know the date.*
5. *be able to text my friend when I am in their house.*
6. *take a photo.*
7. *be able to wake up to an alarm in the morning.*
8. *find my way in the dark.*

Most kids today won't understand the joy of playing with the telephone cord.

Marathon runners don't check their phone for three hours. Well done.

When you are bored send a text to a random phone number saying, "I hid the body, now what?"

Solve most of your problems by not answering your phone.

Interesting that mobile phones these days keep getting thinner and smarter; people the opposite.

Camping out for days waiting for new iPhone releases is a fun way to prepare for your impending homelessness.

Bought a smart phone today and it came with unlimited "Staring at your phone to avoid contact with other people" minutes.

Being in a relationship is the exhausting practice of ceaselessly trying to be more entertaining than a smart phone.

Remember that as a teenager you are at the last stage of your life when you will be happy to hear that the phone is for you. (Fran Lebowitz)

Ever had a mini heart attack when you reach in your pocket and your phone isn't there?

No name, no matter how simple, can be correctly understood over the phone.

Do you keep some people's phone numbers in your phone just so you know not to answer when they call?

There must be some force-field app causing people to brazenly wander into traffic while staring at their phone.

For some people the quickest way to sober up during a night out is to pat your pockets and not feel your phone.

Finally to the fourth ape: hears nobody, sees nobody, speaks to nobody, just looks at his phone.

Sorry I took so long to answer the phone. I was dancing to the ring tone.

The beauty of the telephone is that it lets us talk to people whom we don’t want to meet.

The only use of a landline phone is to find your mobile.

Headphones tie themselves in knots while you're not looking. Proven.

Hmm … Voyager 1 is 8.2 billion miles from Earth and continues to send readings back to us, and I can't get mobile phone reception in my living room?

Remember when phones were stupid and people were smart? Good times.

The weather app on my phone needs to look outside more often.

Smart phone, smart phone on a stick, who has the fairest selfie pic?

My memory? Oh, I traded that in for an iPhone.

If your phone didn't light up so many times to tell you there was low battery it wouldn't have died so quickly.

She was not the sort of person you should put on speaker phone.

Hang out with people who make you forget to look at your phone.

It would be great if exams came with options of 50/50 and phone a friend.

Treat your passwords like a toothbrush. Don't let anyone else use it, and get a new one every twelve months.

Any room is a panic room if you've lost your phone in it.

If you want a sneak preview of the new iPhone just look at your current iPhone and pretend it costs $999 more.

Why did my iPhone suddenly stop working just as the new iPhone came out?

iPhones are so expensive these days if you fall and hear a crack you hope it's your leg.

My phone just filmed a six-hour documentary about life inside my pocket.

If your phone gets wet, try putting it in a bag of dry rice and at night the rice will attract Asians who will fix the phone for you.

Pretty sure the zombie apocalypse started the day smart phones were invented.

Heart pounding, pupils dilated, fingers trembling, dry mouth, sweaty palms, rising feeling of panic. Where has my phone gone?

You know your phone can take pictures of other people too, right? Just checking.

Phone batteries live longer than some relationships these days.

Life is what happens while your phone is charging.

No, officer, I didn't see you in the rear vision mirror. My eyes haven't left my phone for at least four kilometres.

How productive workers are at work is judged by how much battery their cell phone has left when they leave.

Have you noticed it is easier to get out of a marriage than a mobile-phone contract?

Talking on the phone to someone who has children is like talking to someone who has Tourettes.

Putting your phone away and paying attention to those talking to you is called "respect".

When you're calling a woman, you need to call her twice. First time to give her a chance to find the phone in her handbag, the second time for her to actually answer.

OK with cutlery, but which side of the plate does the phone go on?

Hey you! You're driving a car. It isn't a telephone booth, a beauty parlour or a restaurant.

Use of modern phones: 50% to access internet, 20% to text, 15% to take photos, 10% to check the time, 5% to actually call someone.

Eight-year-old's today have Facebook, Twitter, phones, and iPod, but when I was their age, I had a colouring book, crayons, chalk, and imagination.

When setting a voice recognition password for his new phone, a nearby dog barked and ran away. Now he's still looking for the dog to unlock his phone.

Ever been more confused than by predictive text on a dyslexic's phone?

People who spend less time on their smartphones are really mad only because they forgot their charger.

Anyone else become faint and nauseous during even very minor medical procedures, such as making an appointment by phone?

Somehow, hitting the "end call" button on the mobile just doesn't feel nearly as good as the old days when you could slam the phone down on somebody.

Apparently we love our own mobile phones but we hate everyone else's.

A sign at the local mall car park said, "Thieves want your sat nav." I just thought, "Well, they can get lost."

How come wrong numbers are never busy?

Got stuck in traffic for so long the other day that even the phone sat nav said, "Are we nearly there yet?"

Mobile phones are not a sign of power, they're a sign of subservience and are the latest invention in rudeness.

Mobile phones are so convenient that they're an inconvenience.

The mobile has become the adult's transitional object, replacing the toddler's teddy bear for comfort and a sense of belonging.

It's easier for a rich man to ride that camel through the eye of a needle directly into the Kingdom of Heaven, than for some of us to give up our mobile phone.

Dear mobile phone companies, please make an "Unsend my text" option.

Do you mind if I strap your phone to my forehead so I can pretend you're looking at me when I talk?

ANIMAL ANTICS

Pigeons had overrun three churches in town. After much prayer, the elders of the first church determined that the birds were predestined to be there. Who were they to interfere with God's will, they reasoned? Soon, the pigeons multiplied.

The elders of the second church, deciding they could not harm any of God's creatures, humanely trapped the birds and set them free outside of town. One day later, the pigeons were back.

It was only the third church that succeeded in keeping the pests away. The elders baptised the birds and registered them as members of the church. Now they only see them on Christmas and Easter.

What dogs do:

Bark as if no one can hear you.

Catch every ball on the fly.

Wag till you knock something over.

Sleep on a sofa nearby.

Jump like the sky is the limit.

Sit by the fire with friends.

Stay with the people who love you.

Run like the road never ends.

An extensive government study has revealed that the leading cause of cancer in laboratory rats is scientists.

⁓

Sign. Dogs are welcome in this hotel.

We never had a dog that smoked in bed, set fire to the blankets, stole our towels, played the TV too loud, or had a fight with his travelling companion.

No dog ever got drunk and broke up the furniture, so if your dog can vouch for you, his owner, then you are welcome too.

⁓

A dog walks into a butcher shop and the butcher asks, "What do you want?" The dog points to steak in a glass case. "How many pounds?" The dog barks twice.

"Anything else?" The dog points to some pork chops and barks four times. So the butcher wraps up a two-pound steak and four pork chops, and places the bag in the dog's mouth.

He then takes money from a purse tied around the dog's neck, and sees him out. A customer, who has been watching in amazement, follows the dog to a house several blocks away, where it rings the doorbell to be let in.

As the owner appears at the door, the customer says, "What a remarkable dog!"

"Remarkable?" snorts the owner. "This is the second time this week he's forgotten his keys."

⁓

Snake 1: Are we biting, poisonous sort of snake or the crushing, squeezing kind?

Snake 2: We are the crushing squeezing kind. Why?

Snake 1: ' That's good cos I just bit my lip.

~

A grasshopper hops into a bar. The bartender says, "You're quite a celebrity around here. We've even got a drink named after you."

The grasshopper says, "What, you've got a drink named Trevor?"

~

A man walks into a pub and there is a horse behind the bar serving drinks.

He stares at the horse in amazement until the horse says, "What's the matter with you? Haven't you ever seen a horse serving drinks before?

"It's not that," says the man. "I just can't believe the parrot sold up."

ANIMAL ANTICS - Dog vs Cat Controversy - You Decide.

The coldest depth of Hell is reserved for people who abandon kittens. (Robert A Heinlein)

Be thankful pets can't talk; they know way too much.

Scientists tell us that the fastest animal on earth, with a top speed of 70 m/s, is a cow that has been dropped out of a helicopter.

A racehorse is a fast means of redistributing wealth.

Horse racing is just animated roulette.

The horse I bet on was so slow, the jockey kept a diary of the trip.

My horse was so late getting home, he tiptoed into the stable.

One of the worst things that can happen to you in life is to win a bet on a horse at an early age.

CATS

Cats never strike a pose that isn't photogenic. Agree?

No matter how much the cats fight, there always seem to be plenty of kittens. (Abraham Lincoln)

The cat is, above all things, a dramatist.

Cats will amusingly tolerate humans only until someone comes up with a tin opener that can be operated with a paw. (Terry Pratchett)

The training procedure with cats is supposed to be difficult. It's not. Mine had me trained in two days.

Cats have an uncanny ability to blame the family dog for things they destroy.

Cat's motto: No matter what you've done wrong, always try to make it look like the dog did it.

As every cat owner knows, nobody *owns* a cat.

Everything I know I learned from my cat. When you're hungry, eat. When you're tired, nap in a sunbeam. When you go to the vet, pee on your owner.

The phrase domestic cat is an oxymoron.

Dogs believe they are human. Cats believe they are God.

Cats are kindly masters, just so long as you remember your place.

Some people say that cats are sneaky, evil, and cruel. True, and they have many other fine qualities as well.

Cats aren't clean, they're just covered with cat spit.

For you to truly understand rejection, you must first be ignored by a cat.

When my cats aren't happy, I'm not happy. Not because I care about their mood but because I know they're just sitting there thinking up vengeful ways to get even. (Percy Bysshe Shelley)

People who don't like cats were probably mice in an earlier life.

When Rome burned, the emperor's cats still expected to be fed on time.

I gave my cat a bath the other day and they loved it. He sat there, he enjoyed it, it was fun for me. The fur would stick to my tongue, but other than that …

A dog can be our best friend, but a cat will never tell the police where the marijuana is.

Cats can work out mathematically the exact place to sit that will cause most inconvenience. (Pam Brown)

Today's generation are so allergic to everything, future wars will be fought by throwing bags of peanuts and cat hair at each other.

Has your cat walked into the room, stared at something you couldn't see and then run away in a panic? Scary.

I have a dog to provide me with unconditional love but I also have a cat to remind me that I don't deserve it. It's all about balance.

One is never sure, watching two cats washing each other, whether it's affection, the taste, or a trial run for the jugular. (Helen Thomson)

No matter what amazing things you accomplish or how fantastic you are, a cat will always think it is better than you.

The problem with cats is that they get the exact same look on their face whether they see a moth or an axe-murderer.

Today I saw a woman talking to her cat as if it understood. Sheeesh. When I got home, me and my dog had a good laugh about it.

Cat owners need to know that the probability of a cat eating its dinner has absolutely nothing to do with the price of the food placed before it.

A cat is just a pygmy lion that loathes mice, hates dogs, and patronises human beings.

Cat bathing is a martial art.

The cat could very well be man's best friend but would never stoop to admitting it.

A man who carries a cat by the tail learns something he can learn in no other way. (Mark Twain)

"Meow" means "woof" in cat.

Cats will outsmart dogs every time.

The way to get on with a cat is to treat it as an equal - or, even better, as the superior it knows itself to be.

If only cats grew into kittens.

Could anyone, prophet, king or God, convince a thousand cats to do the same thing at the same time? Nah.

Cat owners please note: a cat isn't fussy just so long as you remember he likes his milk in the shallow, rose-patterned saucer, and his fish on the blue plate from which he will take it, and eat it off the floor.

Anyone who believes what a cat tells them deserves all they get.

Cats are intended to teach us that not everything in nature has a function.

If the earth was flat, cats would have pushed everything off of it by now.

Watch Me Pee on This: And Other Poems by Cats.

If cats looked like frogs we'd realize what nasty, cruel little bastards they are. Style. That's what people remember. (Sir Terry Pratchett)

DOGS

Have you ever stopped to think who actually tries dog food to know it has a "newly improved flavour"?

I've tried the carrot and the stick method with my dog but she hates carrots and loves sticks. Please explain.

A psychologist is selling a video that teaches you how to test your dog's IQ. Here's how it works: if you spend $12.99 for the video, your dog is smarter than you.

People say, "If you want loyalty, get a dog," but my dog would abandon me in a dark alley for a pizza crust, so maybe loyalty has layers.

That dog acts like her entire family was murdered by a vacuum cleaner.

Watch a dog and you realise that those who teach us most about humanity are not humans.

Do not make snow angels in a dog park.

A dog is the only friend you can buy for money.

Dogs will give you unconditional love until the day they die. Cats will make you pay for every mistake you have ever made since the day you were born.

If a dog jumps into your lap it is because it is fond of you. A cat will do it only because it is warmer.

Sign: Beware of the dog. The cat is not trustworthy either.

How to view dogs: beagle, German shepherd, poodle, pitbull, labrador.

How to view cats: cat, cat, cat, cat.

Don't accept your dog's admiration as conclusive evidence that you are wonderful.

Be thankful that being socially distant does not include your dog.

One thing his dog and he have in common is they both don't want him to go to work.

You don't get to tell me what to do; you're not my dog.

All dogs are therapy dogs; just some are freelancing.

Feel sorry for people who do not have a dog, because they have to pick up food they drop on the floor.

That five-second rule regarding dropped food doesn't mean much when you have a two-second dog.

Whoever said you can't buy happiness forgot about puppies.

Properly trained, a man can be dog's best friend.

A dog is one of the remaining reasons why some people can be persuaded to go for a walk.

Dogs laugh, but they laugh with their tails.

If you think dogs can't count, try putting three dog biscuits in your pocket and then give him only two of them.

A well-trained dog will make no attempt to share your lunch. He will just make you feel so guilty that you cannot enjoy it unless you share.

We come back from a grocery store with the most amazing haul of chicken, pork and half a cow. Dogs must think we're the greatest hunters on earth.

Dogs teach us a very important lesson in life: the mailman is not to be trusted.

My cats inspire me daily. They inspire me to get a dog.

My dog is worried about the economy because Pedigree food is up to $4.00 a can. That's almost $28.00 in dog money.

If aliens saw us walking our dogs and picking up their poop, who would they think is in charge?

Beware! Dog can't hold its licker.

Every snack you make, every meal you bake, every bite you take … I'll be watching you.

There is no such thing as personal space when you have a dog.

The most affectionate creature in the world is a wet dog. (Ambrose Bierce)

A Chihuahua looks like a dog that is still a long way away.

I sometimes look into the face of my dog and see a wistful sadness and existential angst, when all he is actually doing is slowly scanning the ceiling for flies.

Life is too short to have only one dog.

Don't drink and drive. Your dog will never understand why you left and never came home. (Might make a good commercial.)

For the best seat in the house you'll have to shift the dog.

Free puppies: half cocker spaniel and half sneaky neighbour's dog.

Dogs are better than human beings because they know but do not tell.

Not to brag or anything, but I'm a big deal to my dog.

CONTEMPLATION CORNER

Sometimes I over think things. For example the three things I think of when the doorbell rings, in priority order, are:

1. Murderer.
2. Police telling me someone is dead.
3. The book I ordered about positive thinking.

But my therapist has told me I over think everything, so that's given me something to think about.

Two men sitting talking.

"How are you?"

"I'm fine. Thanks for asking."

"And how is you son? Still unemployed?"

"Yes he is, but he is meditating now."

"What's that?"

"I don't know, but it's better than sitting around doing nothing."

She spent a lot of time on her treadmill contemplating her future because she was going nowhere fast. Also spent time folding laundry and seriously contemplating becoming a nudist, until she remembered what she looked like naked and so kept folding.

Being in the "busy club" brings many "benefits". It tells the world you are very, very important, you have lots on your plate (more than anyone else), lots of people wanting a piece of you (because you are indispensable), lots of work and lots of places you need to be, *but* is it worth it? (Kate Christie)

~

My therapist says my job is too stressful and driven by competition, so she recommended meditation. I think I'm a natural talent. I finished my first 5 minute meditation in under 2 minutes 49 seconds.

~

When she is quiet, those who don't know her look at her and thinks she is shy.

Those who do know her say, OMG she's thinking! Run for your lives!

~

Give yourself a gift of five minutes of contemplation in awe of everything you see around you.

Go outside and turn your attention to the many miracles.

This five-minute-a-day regimen of appreciation and gratitude will help you to focus your life in awe. (Wayne Dyer)

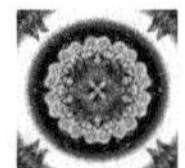 

CONTEMPLATION CORNER

Try to be with someone who makes you forget what it felt like to be sad.

Don't tell me the sky is the limit when there are footprints on the moon.

If you see nothing you could be grateful for, check your pulse.

If you cannot change your mind you cannot change anything. (George Bernard Shaw)

I am who I am and your approval is not needed.

The standard you walk past, is the standard you accept. (David Hurley)

Don't focus on the troubles you have, rather on the troubles you don't have.

If you really want something, you will find a way. If you don't, you will find an excuse.

You cannot build a reputation on what you are going to do.

If you cannot get someone out of your head, maybe they are supposed to be there.

You're responsible for your journey in life, no one else. You have to know the destination to go there. Others can help show you the way, but no one can take you there.

All blame is a waste of time. No matter how much fault you find with another, and regardless of how much you blame him, it will not change you. (Wayne Dyer)

Excuses will always be there for you. Opportunity won't.

Danger. Once you learn to quit, it can become a habit.

The worst thing you can do is nothing.

Start where you are. Use what you have. Do what you can.

If you never had a bad day, how would you know whether you were having a good day?

Do the thing you fear most and the death of fear is certain. (Mark Twain)

When the world says, "Give up," hope whispers, "Try it one more time."

If you can't be content with what you have received, be thankful for what you have escaped.

Do not judge a person's story by the chapter you walked in on.

It's never going to be perfect, so just get it done.

Of all treasures, knowledge is the greatest because it cannot be given away, stolen or consumed. (Carrie Prince)

When I let go of what I am, I become what I might be. (Lao Tzu)

A champion is someone who gets up when they can't.

If you want to go fast, go alone, but if you want to go far, go together.

Don't you find the phrase "Je ne sais quoi" has got a certain something?

Common sense is dead and buried, and what we have today is rare sense.

Living tip: Take what you do seriously but don't take yourself too seriously.

Even the worst that has ever happened to you could have been worse.

Raise your words, not your voice. It is rain that grows flowers, not thunder.

You never know how strong you are until being strong is the only choice you have.

Take care to get what you like, or you will be forced to like what you get. (George Bernard Shaw)

There are three C's in life - chances, choices, change and you must make a choice to take a chance or your life will never change.

You don't have to see the whole staircase, just take the first step.

Everyone has a chapter they don't read out loud.

Confidence is not walking into a room thinking you are better than everyone else, it's walking in and not having to compare yourself to anyone at all.

Education is not something you can finish. (Isaac Asimov)

So far, you've survived 100% of your worst days. This too shall pass.

I wonder if common sense will ever make a comeback.

Life begins at the end of your comfort zone.

No matter how rich, talented or intelligent you are, how you treat animals is all people need to know about you.

Never cut a rope that can be simply untied.

Let him that would move the world, first move himself. (Socrates)

Only those who attempt the absurd can achieve the impossible.

Diligence is the mother of good luck.

You are younger today than you ever will be again. Make use of it for the sake of tomorrow.

There aren't nearly enough crutches in the world for all the lame excuses.

There is nothing wrong with being wrong.

You can shut your eyes but you can't ever shut your mind.

The cure for boredom is books. There is no cure for books.

Growth is painful, change is painful, but nothing is as painful as staying stuck somewhere you don't belong.

Jump and you will find out how to unfold your wings as you fall. (Ray Bradbury)

We are no longer happy as soon as we wish to be happier.

One kind word can warm three winter months. (Japanese proverb)

Life's real failure is when you do not realise how close you were to success when you gave up.

The best remedy for indecision is to begin.

Start from wherever you are with what you've got.

It is by chance that we met, by choice that we became friends.

The future will soon be a thing of the past.

The richest person is not the one who has the most, but the one who needs the least.

Don't confuse what you have a right to do with what's right to do. (William Bennett)

You'll never have this day again so make it count.

The greatest mistake you can make in life is to be continually fearing you will make one.

Muddy waters that are let stand become clear.

Don't be afraid that your life will end, be afraid that it will never begin.

Knowing what is right and not doing it is as bad as knowing what is wrong and doing it.

Everything you've ever wanted is on the other side of fear.

Wonder why people get excited about *virtual* reality yet are not interested in *actual* reality.

You can be the moon and still be jealous of the stars.

You'll never find a rainbow if you are looking down.

Conflict cannot survive without your participation. (Wayne Dyer)

The moment someone tells you that you're not good enough is the moment you know you're better than them.

If you board the wrong train, it is no use running along the corridor in the other direction.

It is better to be able to appreciate things you cannot have than to have things you are not able to appreciate.

Promise a lot and deliver even more.

If people doubt how far you can go, go so far that you cannot hear them any more.

Be kind, for everyone you meet is fighting a harder battle. (Plato)

If you don't like how things are, change it. You are not a tree.

A smile is an inexpensive way to change your looks.

A wife who loses a husband is called a widow. A husband who loses a wife is called a widower. A child who loses his parents is called an orphan. There is no word for a parent who loses a child. That's how awful the loss is.

We must change our minds about those whose minds have changed.

It is the mark of an educated mind to be able to entertain a thought without accepting it. (Aristotle)

If you're going to quit anything, quit being lazy, quit making excuses, and quit waiting for the right time.

365 days, 365 new chances.

What you allow is what will continue.

Men build too many walls and not enough bridges. (Isaac Newton)

You are not what happened to you but rather you are what you choose to become.

Those who never make a mistake take their orders from one who does.

The true measure of a person is what they would do if they knew they would never be caught.

Suggest we shouldn't judge people for the choices they make when we don't know what options they had to choose from.

Our fingerprints last forever on the people we touch.

You are not your mistake. It is what you did, not who you are.

You not only have the right to be an individual, you have an obligation to be one. (Eleanor Roosevelt)

A man cannot be comfortable without his own approval. (Mark Twain)

How long should you try? Until. (Jim Rohn)

Doubt kills more dreams than failure ever will.

It's not who you are that holds you back, it's who you think you're not.

Nobody, but nobody, is too busy. It's just a matter of priorities.

It is never too late to be what you might have been.

You know, nobody ever damaged their eyesight by looking on the bright side.

Never throw mud. You may miss your mark, but you will have dirty hands.

You can never leave footprints that last if you are always walking on tiptoe. Just go for it.

There are times in life when people must know when not to let go. Balloons are designed to teach small children this.

Life is not a matter of holding good cards but of playing a poor hand well. (Robert Louis Stevenson)

Don't be afraid of rejection. It hurts, but you won't die from it.

Don't worry about what people think of you, because you cannot change it.

Failure is an event, never a person.

Don't miss out on something that could be great just because it could also be difficult.

Anyone who has time to whine and complain about something has the time to do something about it.

I always advise people never to give advice. (PG Wodehouse)

If you find a road with no obstacles it probably doesn't lead anywhere.

If it doesn't seem to be worth the effort it probably isn't.

One person with backbone will do more than a thousand with a mere wishbone.

When your life flashes before your eyes, make sure you've got plenty to watch.

Free advice is worth the price.

Even if you fall on your face, you're still moving forward.

You can fail many times, but you are not a failure until you begin to blame someone else.

Many of life's failures are people who did not realise how close they were to success when they gave up.

Do not go where the path may lead; go instead where there is no path and leave a trail. (Ralph Waldo Emerson)

If you've never failed you've never stretched yourself.

Before you reach the top of the ladder, make sure it's leaning against the right wall.

When someone tells you, "You can't," turn around and say, "Watch me!"

There is a difference between giving up and knowing you've had enough.

Motivation is what gets you started but it's habit that keeps you going.

What reason weaves, by passion is undone. (Alexander Pope)

Being bigheaded can be as irritating and as dangerous as being small-minded.

Why should we worry about what others think of us? Do we have more confidence in their opinions than we do our own? (Brigham Young)

None are so empty as those who are full of themselves.

Because of self-doubt, the fear of failure, or laziness, most people usually bite off way less than they can chew.

Four things you can't recover: The stone after the throw. The word after it's said. The occasion after it's missed. The time after it's gone.

The only person you should try to be better than is the person you were yesterday.

If it cost you your peace of mind, you paid too much.

We must all suffer one of two things: the pain of discipline or the pain of regret. (Jim Rohn)

Don't stop when you're tired; stop when you're done.

My parents used to take me to the pet shop and tell me it was a zoo.

Real friends are the ones who survive transitions between address books.

The difference between who you are and what you want to be is what you do.

Greeting cards are useful when you care enough to send the very best, but don't care enough to actually write something.

The less you talk, the more you're listened to.

Why is it that no matter how busy we are, we always find time to worry.

Never interrupt anyone doing what couldn't be done while they are doing it.

When everything seems to be against you, remember that an airplane takes off against the wind, not with it. (Henry Ford)

Morality is an instinctive sense of right and wrong that tells some people how everyone else should behave.

Millions saw apples fall, but Newton was the only one to ask why.

If ever you feel you are less than adequate look around and you'll feel a lot better.

Bless the cynics because they see things as they are, not as they ought to be. (Ambrose Bierce)

Those who want to lead an orchestra must turn their back on the crowd.

A positive mind finds a way it can be done; a negative mind looks for all the ways it can't be done. (Napoleon Hill)

You will never plough a field if you only turn it over in your mind. (Irish proverb)

If you can't stop thinking about it, buy it.

The expert in anything was once a beginner.

As they waste their breath complaining, they need to remember someone out there is breathing their last. Be grateful.

People suffer more than necessary if they suffer before it is necessary.

Being prejudiced is a great time-saver that enables you to form opinions without bothering to get the facts.

It's not what you look at that matters, it's what you see. (Henry David Thoreau)

If you don't hope to win you've already lost. (Simon Bolivar)

Stand up for what is right, even if you're standing alone.

A QUANTUM OF QUAINT QUIRKY QUIPS

There are those rare individuals who, while babies in their bassinets, were visited by a strange gypsy woman who cast a spell over them and thereafter for the rest of their lives they are able to wake up each morning with all their mental and physical motors running at full speed.

Don't know what that is like? Neither do I.

~

I saw my mate Charlie this morning. He's only got one arm, bless him.

I shouted, "Where you off to Charlie?"

He said, "I'm off to change a light bulb."

Well I just cracked up, couldn't stop laughing, then said, "That's gonna be a bit awkward isn't it with only one arm?"

"Not really," he said. "I still have the receipt, you insensitive bastard."

~

The salesman sensed he was close to clinching the deal and boasted, "Yes, this little machine will do half your work for you."

"Great," replied the customer, "I'll take two."

~

Your time spent in the shower:

25% Daydreaming.

25% Summoning up courage to turn the water off and step out into the cold air.

20% Turning in a circle to maintain even hot water distribution.

10% Catching water in your mouth and spitting it out.

10% Contemplating the hardest decisions of life.

7% Washing hair.

3% Washing other body parts.

"What's your name, son?" the principal asked his student.

The kid replied, "D-d-d-dav-dav-david, sir."

"Do you have a stutter?" the principal asked.

The student answered, "No, sir, my dad has a stutter, but the guy who registered my name was a real smart alec heartless prick."

Police officer: “Sir, I don’t understand You lost the credit card a year ago, why are you reporting it now?”

Him: “The thief wasn’t spending nearly as much as my wife used to…”

Police officer: “But why report it now?”

Him: “I think the thief’s wife got hold of it now.”

Think of a number between one and ten. Multiply it by nine and subtract one. Now shut your eyes. It's dark isn't it?

A QUANTUM OF QUAINT QUIRKY QUIPS

Unicorns are real. It's just they are grey and fat and we call them rhinos.

How fast does a zebra have to run before it looks grey?

Some call it multi-tasking, but it is really what I'm doing while I try to remember what I was doing in the first place.

I was asked to name all the prime ministers. I thought they all had names.

Dont you hait it wen stoopid peeple spel stuff rong?

The three hardest things to say are, 1. I was wrong. 2. I need help. 3. Worcestershire Sauce.

You are only as good as your last haircut.

My "give a damn" is broken, and they don't make spare parts to fix it.

We would not deem life too short if we always remembered that we do not have to watch television.

Sorry for being late. I got caught up enjoying my last few minutes of not being here.

Today is one of those days when even my coffee will need a coffee.

Wear a balaclava to bed so if there's a home invasion, they'll think you are part of the team.

I'll have a double cappuccino, half-caf, non-fat milk, with enough foam to be aesthetically pleasing, but not so much that it would leave a moustache.

Men fall in love with what they see, and women with what they hear, which is why women wear makeup and men lie.

The planet owes me. Every day I spend all day converting oxygen into carbon dioxide.

I hate standing in lines. I wish this woman would hurry up and pick a suspect already.

Nothing saves money like being antisocial.

The hospital you are born in is the only building you leave without entering.

If insanity is doing the same thing over and over again and expecting a different result, then stop cleaning the house.

Tact is for people who are not witty enough to be sarcastic.

There are no bad photos. That's just how you do look sometimes.

Grab your dumbrella 'cos it's really stupid out there today.

Forgive and forget? No, I'm not Jesus nor do I have Alzheimer's.

I just got my doctor's test results and I'm really upset. Turns out, I'm not gunna be a doctor.

As I get older, I remember all the people I lost along the way. Maybe a career as a tour guide was not the right choice.

It's important to have a good vocabulary. If I had known the difference between the words "antidote" and "anecdote", one of my good friends would still be alive.

The guy who stole my diary just died. My thoughts are with his family.

Welcome back to Plastic Surgery Anonymous. Nice to see so many new faces here today!

Her backside was so big it began to affect the tides.

Sometimes I question my sanity, and occasionally it replies.

Your mother told you if you cannot say anything nice don't say anything at all. And some people wonder why you are so silent around them.

When someone says to me "great minds think alike", I think, you dirty little bastard.

If you see someone at the movies buying candy, soft drink and a big popcorn, they are a drug dealer because there is no other explanation for that level of income.

Revenge is not her style, but accidents happen.

What if your pillow could capture your dreams and when you wake up you could plug it into your phone and watch them all over again.

Most of my exercise today is shaking my head in disbelief.

Currently our ears are carrying our headphones, sun glasses and face mask. Ears are the new purse.

Her hair lounged on her shoulders like an anesthetized cocker spaniel.

You get to an age when the things you used to care to do, you no longer care to do, but you really do care that you don't care to do them anymore.

I have OCD and ADD so everything has to be perfect but not for too long.

You're fat, but I won't sugar coat that because you'd eat that too.

Once I lose this weight I'll be thin enough to go to the gym.

Not many people know this. The symbol at the top left of your keyboard, ~, is called a tilde. You're welcome.

Lord, help me to be the person my psychiatrist medicates me to be.

A truly worthwhile and satisfying career - nail polish namer.

Dear Karma, here is a list of people you missed.

Some people die at twenty-five and aren't buried until seventy-five. (Benjamin Franklin)

They say beauty is in the eye of the beholder, but us bee keepers are a lot less popular with the ladies than you might think.

How can you tell me to never say never when you just said never?

To gain weight, takeaway pizza. To lose weight, take away pizza.

Pubs are the official sun block of Australians.

Don't be afraid to die fat. That's your pallbearers' worry.

On the bright side, selfie sticks are also lightning rods.

Loquacity: a disorder which renders the sufferer unable to curb his tongue when you wish to talk. (Ambrose Bierce)

My three favourite things are eating my family and not using commas.

Instant gratification takes too long.

The only thing you have to fear is fear itself - and spiders.

They told me I'd never be any good at poetry because I'm dyslexic, but so far I've made two jugs and a vase!

There's a fine line between hyphenated words.

Just had an argument with my friend Tristan, or stan stan stan for the commoners. (You smart people grinned didn't you.)

The Japanese flag is really a pie chart of how afraid they are of Godzilla.

Sunglasses allow you to stare at people without getting caught. Like Facebook, only in real life.

Customer service: "And how does your name appear on your credit card?" "I'd say about 11 pt Arial Bold."

Announce: thirty grams or a sixteenth of a pound. (You have to be over fifty years of age to understand this).

Three midgets walk into a mini-bar.

Three out of four voices in my head say try to sleep, while the other wants to know if penguins have knees.

Paper cut: a tree's final moment of revenge.

There is no government like *no* government.

The sun rose slowly, as if it wasn't sure it was worth all the effort.

My wife sent me a text saying, "Your great," so I responded with, "You're great too." She has been wandering around with a smile on her face. Should I let her know I was just correcting her grammar or just let it be?

The chemical composition of Holy Water is H_2OMG.

"Angling" is the word given to fishing by people who can't fish.

Stars cannot shine without ~~darkness~~. Sorry, nuclear fusion.

You are now aware that you can't say Irish wristwatch three times quickly. Try it.

Sometimes Google should just come back with a message that says, "Trust me, you don't want to know."

Actually, Officer, if you factor in the earth's rotation, we were all speeding. Didn't work but worth a try.

We all live for two reasons. 1. We were born. 2. We haven't died yet.

An argument is two people trying to get in the last word first.

Every meal I didn't have to cook myself is the best meal I've ever had.

Whoops: an exclamation that translates roughly into "get a mop and bucket."

Anyone here with one leg? I have a ton of socks you can have.

Could toilet paper manufacturers please make the last six sheets courtesy red?

To kill a spider get a piece of tissue paper, approach it slowly, and, very carefully, burn the house down.

If you have a bald spot in your lawn let the grass around it grow really long and then do a comb-over.

I'm not easily distracted I ... Hey look! Jewellery!

Nothing is made in vain, but the fly came near it.

Average is the best of the worst and the worst of the best.

End all your sentences with "just saying ..." because ending them with "you dickhead" would probably be considered offensive.

Homonyms are a reel waist of thyme.

I wouldn't say he is stupid. He is, but I wouldn't say it.

Ever notice that the letters "T" and "G" are far too close together on a keyboard. This is why I'll never be ending an e-mail with the phrase "Regards" ever again.

Save the cost of a sky dive by zooming in on Google Earth really, really fast.

"Alas" is the early Victorian term for "Shit".

When you turn off the computer by holding down the power button, it feels like choking it to death. You know it does.

How dare you incinerate that I don't know big words.

Just completed my 127th OCD awareness course.

Noah, we could have sworn you said the ark wasn't leaving till 5. *Sincerely, Unicorns.*

In answer to whether the car indicators are working: "Now it is, now it isn't, now it is, now it isn't …"

They must have named the orange before the carrot.

Russian dolls are so full of themselves.

The person who invented the umbrella was going to call it the "brella" but he hesitated.

Words can't express how much I hate World Emoji Day.

You've made a happy man very old.

Having finally finished my 40,000 piece jigsaw, it reads: "Get a life, you poor, sad bastard."

This one isn't funny; just keep reading.

To get quick service at Bunning's, try to start a chainsaw.

Just bought a JVC LCD 4K 3D UHD TV. The rest of the alphabet was out of stock.

The height of embarrassment is when two sets of eyes meet through a keyhole.

Vegans believe meat eaters and butchers are gross, but those who sell you fruits and vegetables are grocer.

The world is a globe, so the farther you sail, the closer to home you are. (Terry Pratchett)

The boomerang is Australia's chief export (and then import).

The phrase "Don't take this the wrong way" has a zero percent success rate.

When you have nothing to say, say nothing.

Ever thought that the perfect gift for a man who has everything is a burglar alarm?

I tried counting sheep so I can fall asleep but that got boring, so I started talking to the shepherd instead.

Just wanted you to know somebody cares. Not me, but somebody.

The next time a spammer calls just answer it and say, "Hello Queensland sperm bank. You squeeze it - we freeze it!" See what happens.

Google Earth: helping stalkers since 2004.

Ever thought about this? A bird in the hand makes blowing your nose difficult.

In my claim the insurance man told me I was covered for falling off the roof but not for hitting the ground.

I would give my right arm to be a pianist.

When there is nothing more to be said he'll still be saying it.

Double negatives are a no-no.

The important thing to remember is not to forget.

Glitter is the herpes of the arts and crafts world 'cos you just can't get rid of it once its on you.

Eighty percent of Japanese women admit to having faked origami.

My life is so full of surprises, nothing surprises me any more.

When you think all the way back to being sperm, we are all winners.

Where is the chase and how do I cut to it?

The height of confidence is standing up in a hammock.

Dating tip: if she hasn't kissed you by the third date, she's there for the food.

She always wore a necklace so she could know when she was upside down.

A perfect summer day is when the sun is shining, the breeze is blowing, the birds are singing, and the lawnmower is broken.

Militant feminists, I take my hat off to them. They don't like that. (Milton Jones)

Life, noun.: A whim of several billion cells to be you for a while.

To make millions, invent an app that deletes your memberships right before the free trials run out.

Lysdexia is a speech impediment we learn to live with.

When she put her purse on the passenger seat the passenger seatbelt light came on. Time to clean out her purse?

Wrap all your Christmas presents in bubble wrap - it's like two gifts in one.

Live each day as if it is your last. Most days you will be wrong.

Jellyfish have existed as a species for five hundred million years, surviving just fine without a brain. That gives hope to quite a few people.

Chocolate doesn't ask any questions. Chocolate simply understands.

Funny that you can't spell "slaughter" without "laughter".

I used to think that you were a pain in the neck. My opinion of you has dropped significantly lower since then.

I wouldn't exactly say I'm lazy, but it's a good thing that breathing is a reflex.

I never read any instructions. I just press buttons until it does what I want.

Married women face a significantly lower risk of kidnapping. Nobody can be certain that the ransom would actually be paid.

Some people's X-rays actually look much better than their photographs.

Cheese is milk's leap toward immortality.

You couldn't get a clue during the clue-mating season in a field full of horny clues if you smeared your body with clue musk and did the clue-mating dance.

Don't eat French fish - it's Poisson.

I'm sorry, fellow student, I don't know where the "liberry" is.

Common sense is not a gift, it is a punishment, because you have to deal with all the idiots who don't have it.

When I say "I'll think about it" it means I'll forget it until you bring it up again.

Sometimes you get and sometimes you get got.

I don't have a bucket list but my f*it list is a mile long.**

On a scale of 1,2,3,4,5,6,7,8,9,10 how OCD are you?

Mathematical fact: you can only be twice someone's age once.

One benefit of living alone is you don't need to buy toothpaste.

Happy tip: adopt a retired drug dog to help find fun friends at parties.

Once you start to read between the lines, you realise that all books are really the same.

For a detective, a surprise party is the ultimate insult.

When you have time, why not learn all the names for lettuce?

She's going to name her next pet Peeve.

I hate jokes that rely on visual imagery. I've had it right up to here with them.

This Male Order Bride is the worst and most expensive typo I've ever paid for.

You're the only one - Valentine's Day cards on sale: two for $5.

After the divorce, before you leave the house release three rats free in the house with 1, 2, and 4 written on their backs.

If you are God's gift to women I hope he kept the receipt.

Over 90% of the stuff on Wikipedia is fake, is an article on Wikipedia.

If I had to describe myself in three words, I would say: "Not very good at maths."

The inventor of the USB stick has died, and at his funeral they gently lowered the coffin, then pulled it back up, turned it the other way, then lowered it again.

My teacher used to say I wasn't very observant but, to be honest, that was his/her opinion.

A group of bad spellers got together and formed an onion.

Tip: you have to get to local Kleptomaniacs Anonymous meetings early before all the seats are taken.

For some, when you lose your "khakis" you've lost a pair of pants. For others, when they lose their "khakis" they can't start their car.

Successfully finished Rubik's cube. Waiting for the paint to dry now.

Wearing socks is an easy way to get the mopping done.

Eleventeen percent of people make up words.

All odd numbers have the letter "e" in them. Not many people know this.

You just checked some of them out didn't you?

The first half of Lolita is hilarious.

My grandkids say they want a cat for Xmas. Normally I do turkey but, hey, if it makes them happy!

I have an angel on one shoulder, the devil on the other, and I also have a deaf ear.

As far as I'm concerned, the word "whom" was invented to make everyone sound like a butler.

Electricity is just organised lightning.

Bald people shouldn't wear polo neck jumpers - they just end up looking like a roll-on deodorant.

What I'm looking for is a blessing not in disguise.

Advertising promotes that most improved things can be improved even further.

There are II types of people in the world: those who understand Roman numerals and those who don't.

Thongs are fun because every time you take a step it's like a high-five for your feet.

Have enough sense to know ahead of time when your skills will not extend to wall papering.

Humour is simply a funny way of being serious.

Dry clean only means it will never be washed.

This is a feminist book store. There is no humour section.

Some talk to you in their free time, while others free their time to talk to you. Learn how to tell the difference.

There is no angry way to say "bubbles".

Maturity involves turning an insult into a feedback.

Obsessed, a word used by the lazy to describe the dedicated.

She used her last Post-It Note and has no idea how to remind herself to get more.

If actions are stronger than words, why is the pen mightier than the sword?

Hear no evil, see no evil, and speak no evil and you'll never get a job working for a tabloid newspaper.

ORGANISM ... you read that wrong the first time didn't you?

So I'm at the wailing wall, standing there like a moron, with my harpoon.

Hundreds of years ago, before guns, did they use a bow and arrow to start a race? Just wondering.

If you can read this I'm not impressed. Most people can read.

It surely can't be a coincidence that Alexander the Great and Kermit the Frog share the same middle name.

I went to the toilet without my phone and found there are 118 tiles on the floor and the longest word on a shampoo bottle is:

"methylchloroisothiazolinone".

Don't confuse Pavlov and Pavlova, or you'll have salivating ballerinas and pirouetting dogs. (Ashleigh Brilliant)

These days if the waitress doesn't have a visible tattoo the restaurant is usually too expensive.

I thought the one liner I was typing here was not that clever or funny and you the reader would agree, so I deleted it.

Spelling errors are to be avoided, otherwise your whole post is urined.

Not many people know that flames don't have shadows.

Went to Rome the other day. It got me thinking, what did Michelangelo do with the other fifteen chapels?

I can't find my hide-and-seek manual.

If you can't read this, you're illiterate.

We must really thympathise with people who have lisps.

You know that feeling when you meet someone and your heart skips a beat. That's arrhythmia and you can die from that.

That girl who sells seashells by the seashore is a moron.

On the Canary Islands there is not one canary, and on the Virgin Islands the same thing; not a single canary there either.

Dear Autocorrect, at no time have I ever meant "Ducking".

For some fun, at the supermarket drop cucumbers and KY Jelly into random people's trolleys.

We've got to find a way to stop the driver of that bus that everyone keeps getting thrown under.

A paperclip is really a staple for people with commitment issues.

Anyone who despises himself will still respect himself as a despiser. WTF?

Large crystal ball for sale. Only $50, but you will haggle me down and buy it for $35.

There's one thing that I can't stand when I'm pissed, and that's up.

Dryer lint is the cremated remains of all missing socks.

Pollen is actually "plant sperm" so hay fever is an STD.

Start a group meeting at your home for people with OCD. Even though you don't have it, one person is bound to want to clean your house.

It's racial profiling when a waiter in a Chinese restaurant gives me a fork.

T-shirts I own: 50. T-shirts I wear: 5. T-shirts I'm prepared to dump: 0.

Every sock lost in the dryer comes back as an extra Tupperware lid.

Have completed the first item on my bucket list ... I got the bucket.

The batteries in my electric toothbrush died before I finished so I've never sympathised more with women.

A giraffe in a top hat walks into a bar and orders six martinis, and shame on you for wanting a punch line. This giraffe needs help.

Auto-correct can to be your worst enema.

If you see an autobiography for sale in the book store just flip to the "About the author section" and it's done. Next?

Once I want the username and password prompt to say, "Close enough."

If spiders ever come to the realisation that people are terrified of them, we're buggered.

The man who invented Velcro has died. RIP.

Queues exist only when you join them.

Burglars note: due to the rising price of ammunition I will not be able to provide a warning shot.

Watching TV always reminds us of why we don't watch TV.

Whenever you see someone in a Smart Car, expect to see a kid with a remote control nearby.

Would it hurt you to walk another three metres and put the shopping trolley back where it belongs?

Science fiction is fairy tales for nerds.

Are you not sure if you understand ambiguity?

Most people do not mind dying, as long as that does not happen today.

The news said heavy snow had fallen so I've just picked some up - it wasn't that heavy.

The other line always moves faster until you get in it.

He is so short he has to stand on a box to kick a duck in the arse.

A pessimist is one who feels bad when he feels good for fear he'll feel worse when he feels better.

Dear sneeze, If you're gonna happen, happen. Don't put a stupid look on my face and leave.

Being an adult is like folding a fitted sheet. No one really knows how.

What a sense of achievement when you parallel park without turning down the radio.

I'm against picketing, but I don't know how to show it. (Mitch Hedberg)

QUESTIONS DESPERATELY IN NEED OF ANSWERS

Three friends went to a café and had coffee and a sandwich for which they paid $10 each. The waiter took the $30 to the manager, who said seeing they were regular customers he'd give $5 back and asked the waiter to return the $5.

The waiter, being a little light-fingered, put $2 in his pocket and gave each of the friends $1 back. So effectively the people had paid $9 each for their meal. True.

Now, the problem is, 3 x $9 = $27, plus the $2 the waiter has is $29.

So where did the missing $1 go?

A young boy enters a barber shop and the barber whispers to his customer, "This is the dumbest kid in the world. Watch while I prove it to you."

The barber puts a dollar bill in one hand and two twenty cent pieces in the other, then calls the boy over and asks, "Which do you want, son?" The boy takes the two twenty-cent pieces and leaves.

"What did I tell you?" said the barber. "That kid never learns!"

Later, when the customer leaves, he sees the same young boy coming out of the ice-cream shop

"Hey, son, may I ask you a question? Why did you take the twenty-cent pieces instead of the dollar bill?"

The boy licked his cone and replied, "Because the day I take the dollar the game is over!"

Biology prac. Challenge: create life. Estimate the differences in subsequent human culture if this form of life had developed one hundred million years earlier, with special attention to its probable effect on the Australian Parliamentary system. Prove your thesis.

Question? Can this be done? (Could be a PhD in it for you.)

A policeman stopped a guy for speeding. He said, "Do you know how fast you were going?"

"I was trying to keep up with traffic," the guy replied.

The cop said, "But there is no traffic."

"That's how far behind I am."

On another occasion, a policeman pulls over a driver. "What's your name?"

"Whitehall."

Policeman:" Where you from?"

"Blackall."

Policeman: "What sort of car is this?"

"Vauxhall."

Policeman: "What have you got in the boot?"

"Nothin'."

~

If one doctor doctors another doctor, does the doctor who doctors the doctor doctor the way the doctor he is doctoring doctors? Or does the doctor doctor the way the doctor who doctors doctors?

~

If womb is pronounced "woom" and tomb is pronounced "toom" shouldn't bomb be pronounced "boom"?

~

Now don't forget to find the missing $1 from above. 

QUESTIONS DESPERATELY IN NEED OF ANSWERS

Does my dog only bring back my ball because he thinks I like throwing it?

Is it possible to be totally partial?

Ever wonder how long you'd be on hold if your call wasn't important to them?

How do you tell the difference between Facebook and the Cartoon Network?

Why do you have to pay full price for Swiss cheese?

Is it true that women only wear high heels to work so they don't have to help move stuff?

If you watch an Apple store get robbed, are you an iWitness?

If all is not lost, where the hell is it?

What is the "nog" in eggnog?

If they use crash test dummies to test things, how do they test crash test dummies?

How come believers get possessed by demons but atheists never do?

Why are Zoey and Zoe pronounced the same way but Joey and Joe aren't?

Why don't they make a remote control to find remote controls?

How many times have you rotated the switch trying to figure out if the ceiling fan is speeding up or slowing down?

What is a wet sense of humour as distinct from a dry sense of humour?

Ever wonder why Chinese restaurants don't serve breakfast?

Has anyone tried to unplug and plug back in the government?

Why is it considered necessary to nail down the lid of a coffin?

Why doesn't glue stick to the inside of the bottle? Science needs to know.

Why do they call it a TV set when you only get one?

Why do people who know the least know it the loudest?

Why do croutons come in airtight packages? Aren't they just stale bread to begin with?

If the universe is everything, and scientists say that the universe is expanding, what is it expanding into?

Why do people try to straighten their glasses with grimaces?

Why did you have to learn what a rhombus is? Literally nothing in this world is rhombus shaped.

What do you call a bunch of keys found in a drawer whose purpose has long been forgotten and which can now be used only for dropping down people's backs as a cure for nose bleeds?

Whoever put the word fun in funeral?

Why is it that advertisements for clocks and watches always show the time as 10:10?

Why is it called a building when it's already built?

If crying doesn't make the sad things better, then why do we do it?

How did "Rub a Dub Dub, Three Men in a Tub" ever become a nursery rhyme?

What would happen if you poured self-raising flour on an orphan?

If steroids are illegal for athletes shouldn't Photoshop be illegal for models?

Why aren't Audi A3s twice the size of Audi A4s like paper is?

Where can you find a tax accountant who's not afraid of prison?

Why is there enough bitumen to make speed humps, but not enough to fill the pot holes?

Why do all the beautiful women with blond hair dye their roots brown?

In movies, why is it that all car chases eventually crash through a fruit stand?

Prison counts as a gated community, right?

Why do birds wake up and spend two hours asking each other where the sun is?

How do you develop the nerve and lack of guilt not to tip?

We name cyclones, why not earthquakes?

It has been proven that doing the moonwalk is the only way to look cool while wiping dog crap off your shoe.

Why are the first tissues the hardest to get out of the box? I just need one, not ten.

What was the first person to dance trying to do?

Is it wishful thinking that the next big trend in music might be talent?

Why is it that they have a loud conversation on their mobile phone and then give us dirty looks for listening to everything they say?

Jack and Jill were both idiots. Who in the hell goes *up* a hill to find water?

How do you tell people you aren't in denial?

Is there another word for synonym?

Why do I have to press 1 for English when they are just going to transfer me to someone I cannot understand anyway?

If one is not to talk to strangers how is one to make friends?

Abbreviations have fewer syllables than the word or phrase they replace so why does w.w.w have nine while world wide web has only three?

Is it possible to have an awkward silence in sign language?

Why do people say tuna fish when they don't say beef animal or chicken bird?

Are they still bad habits if you like them?

Why does quicksand work slowly?

Why do engineers make the joints in the footpath too far apart for one step and too close for two?

Why don't computer companies design a keyboard with a removable crumb tray, like a toaster?

How do germs know they have to wait five seconds before attaching to the food that just fell on the floor?

Why are Adam and Eve always depicted with belly buttons?

If an octopus loses a tentacle does it become a heptopus?

Has anyone actually ever seen a storm in a tea cup?

Do twins ever recognise that one of them was unplanned?

Does an animal coroner during an autopsy on cats have to check the "curiosity" box under "cause of death"?

Which is longer, a microwave minute or a treadmill minute?

What are birds so excited about at 5 am?

At what age is it appropriate to tell your dogs they are adopted?

Why is it is so much easier for most people to ignore an insult than it is for them to ignore a compliment?

Why do they call that funny little statue a bust when it stops right before the part of the body that it's named after?

Why do prostitutes charge per hour? What are we supposed to do for the other fifty-seven minutes?

Why do many woman always feel judged when buying a cucumber?

Has science explained why you have to walk around the house when on the phone?

Where is the unsubscribe button on adulthood?

Does most Braille on public signs say: "How did you know this was here?"

Why is it easier to stay awake until 6 am than to wake up at 6 am?

Respect has to be earned, so how come blocking traffic, damaging businesses and getting people frustrated is supposed to build respect for their cause? Just asking.

Whatever happened to the hole in the ozone layer? Did global warming heat it shut?

Ever spend time in meetings wondering how they got that huge meeting table through the door?

Why put the extra "r" in February, and who thought up the spelling for Wednesday?

Why are there never any drugs with good side effects?

Why would someone put down their needle anywhere near a haystack?

Why do people choose their insurance providers based on whose TV commercial is funnier?

How long does it take a giraffe to throw up?

Which zodiac sign is the most likely to think astrology is nonsense?

Does anybody uses Head and Shoulders to wash their shoulders?

If someone with multiple personalities threatens to kill himself, is it considered a hostage situation?

Can anyone explain why it is necessary for the first square of a roll of toilet paper to be glued down?

Why call them anti-anxiety prescriptions instead of relaxatives?

Does Brazil have a wax museum?

If cockroaches can survive ice ages, nuclear war and chemical warfare, what the hell is in a can of Mortein?

If a word in the dictionary were misspelled, how would we know?

Why do people with bad breath always have to tell me secrets?

Just wondering, how do they signal Batman during daytime?

If a dentist makes his money off people with unhealthy teeth, why should I trust a toothpaste that four out of five dentists recommend?

Why put a new word into the dictionary just because enough stupid people use it?

Why do people assume he's got a good personality just because he's ugly?

Why can't the house clean itself? It seems to get dirty by itself!

Who actually clicks on the "No, I am not over 18" links on "adult" pages?

If breast/penis enlargement cream worked, wouldn't your hands get bigger?

Does your face ever hurt from making that look of concern as you pretend to listen?

Why do interior decorators do things to your house they wouldn't dream of doing to their own?

Why is it that when opportunity knocks on your door, it knocks only once, but temptation leans on the damn door bell?

Anyone going to tell TV's Funniest Home Videos about YouTube?

Why is it that when you are ignoring a phone call, the phone seems to ring longer than usual?

Do bomb disposal technicians take four hours to open each of their Christmas presents?

Why do people holding a device capable of using Google ask me stupid questions?

Why do paper-towel dispensers in public restrooms give you just enough to keep your hands slightly damp?

Has it occurred to anyone that if you can organise that many people to protest, you can organise that many people to Clean Up Australia?

Why is there a song you hate but your brain says that it has memorised it and intends to play it all day in your head?

Why do truck deliveries that normally take one day take five when you are waiting for the truck?

Why can't historians let bygones be bygones?

Why is it that the average person thinks someone else is the average person?

Found that dollar from p. 208 yet?

UNIVERSAL LAWS YOU MAY HAVE FORGOTTEN

Mrs. Smith goes to the doctor's office to collect her husband's test results.

The lab tech says to her, "I'm sorry, but there has been a bit of a mix-up and we have a problem. When we sent the samples from your husband to the lab, the samples from another Mr Smith were sent as well and we are now uncertain which one is your husband's. Frankly, that's either bad or terrible."

"What do you mean?"

"Well, one Mr Smith has tested positive for Alzheimer's disease and the other for an STD. We can't tell which is your husband."

"That's terrible! Can we do the test over?" asked Mrs Smith.

"Normally, yes, but Medicare says they won't pay for these expensive tests more than once."

"Well, what am I supposed to do now?"

"Medicare recommends that you drop your husband off in the middle of the city. If he finds his way home, don't sleep with him."

A lawyer died and arrived at the pearly gates. To his dismay, there were thousands of people ahead of him in line to see St Peter. To his surprise, St Peter left his desk at the gate and came down the long line to where the lawyer was and greeted him warmly.

Then St Peter and one of his assistants took the lawyer by the hands and guided him up to the front of the line, and into a comfortable chair by his desk.

The lawyer said, "I don't mind all this attention, but what makes me so special?"

St Peter replied, "Well, I've added up all the hours for which you billed your clients, and by my calculation you must be about 193 years old!"

The policeman tells the accused, "I have some good news and some bad news."

"What's the bad news?" asks the accused.

"The bad news is, your blood is all over the crime scene, and the DNA tests prove you did it."

"What's the good news?"

"Your cholesterol is normal."

Judge (to young witness): "Do you know what would happen to you if you told a lie?"

Witness: "Yes. I would go to hell."

Judge: "Is that all?"

Witness: "Isn't that enough?"

"Doctor, how many of your autopsies have you performed on dead people?"

Witness: "All of them. The live ones put up too much of a fight."

Q: Isn't it a fact that you have been running around with another woman?

A: Yes, it is, but you can't prove it!

UNIVERSAL LAWS YOU MAY HAVE FORGOTTEN

A Woman's Rule of Thumb: if it has tires or testicles, you're going to have trouble with it.

Accountancy Discoveries: Trial balances don't. Working capital doesn't. Liquidity tends to run out. Return on investments won't.

Alice's Discovery: at a bargain sale, the suit or dress that you like best and that fits you is the one not in the sale.

Arrival Law: those who live closest arrive latest.

Automotive Truism: the little space between the driver's seat and the centre console in a car will fit any object that can possibly be dropped, but will not fit a hand.

Axiom: you always find something in the last place you look.

Babcock's Law: if it can be borrowed and it can be broken, you *will* borrow it and you *will* break it.

Biondi's Law: if your project doesn't work, look for the part you didn't think was important.

Boulding's Conclusion: mathematics brought rigor to economics. Unfortunately, it also brought mortis.

Budgeting Law: under current practices, both expenditures and revenues rise to meet each other, no matter which one may be in excess.

Buy Online Hypothesis: If you don't write to complain, you'll never receive your order. If you do write, you'll receive the merchandise before your angry letter reaches its destination.

Byrne's Law: in any electrical circuit, appliances and wiring will burn out to protect fuses.

Camping Edict: start erecting the tent before you start drinking.

Cert's Observation: there is an old proverb that says just about whatever you want it to.

Chamber's Theorem: everything tastes more or less like chicken.

Cheops' Law: nothing ever gets built on schedule or within budget.

Child's Revelation: an unbreakable toy is good for breaking other toys.

Chubb's Rule: the slowest checker is always at the quick-check-out lane.

Climatology Decree: wind velocity increases directly with the cost of the hairdo.

Cohen's Law: people are divided into two groups, - the righteous and the unrighteous, and it's the righteous who do the dividing.

Correction Rule: when an error has been detected and corrected, it will be found to have been correct in the first place.

Coved's Discovery: All probabilities are 50%. Either a thing will happen or it won't.

Creb's Axiom: the search for someone to blame is always successful.

Darwin's Observation: nature will tell you a direct lie if she can.

Diet Edict: food that tastes the best has the highest number of calories.

Dirt Observation: the mud that won't come off on the doormat immediately adheres to the carpet.

Dolly Parton Observation: the bigger they are, the harder it is to see your shoes.

Economist's Corollary: if on an actuarial basis there is a 50/50 chance that something will go wrong, it will actually go wrong nine times out of ten.

Ester's Law of Annoyance: when you're not in a hurry, the traffic light will turn green as soon as your vehicle comes to a complete stop.

Evening Ritual: exit Facebook, close laptop, get into bed, unlock phone, check Facebook.

Exam Conclusions: if given an open- book exam, you will forget to take the book or, if you are given a take-home exam, you will forget where you live.

Exam Maxim: 80% of the final exam will be based on the one lecture you missed and the one book you didn't read.

First Law of Bridge: it's always the partner's fault.

Fifth Law for Husbands: never try to guess your wife's size. Just buy her anything marked "petite" and hold on to the receipt.

Fishing Edict: the more elaborate and costly the equipment, the greater chance of having to stop at the fish market on the way home.

Fossil Fuel Truism: the level of petrol in your car fuel tank depends entirely on how late you are.

Frustration Theorem: one cannot make an omelette without breaking eggs - but unlimited eggs can be broken without making a decent omelette.

Fumble's Maxim: when you want to unlock a door but only have one hand free, the keys will be in the opposite pocket.

Glass's Law: if it says "one size fits all", it doesn't fit anyone.

Green's Law: usefulness is inversely proportional to reputation for being useful. (TV Infomercials)

Grocery Bag Law: the chocolate you planned to eat on the way home from the market is hidden at the bottom of the grocery bag.

Gunter's Law of Air Travel: the strength of the turbulence is directly proportional to the temperature of your coffee.

Granddad's Postulate: you never really learn to swear until you learn to drive.

Healthy Eating Rule: the longer the shelf-life the shorter yours.

Hodges' Observation: the problem with government is that it scratches where there ain't no itch.

Household Analysis: cleaning anything involves making something else dirty, but anything can get dirty without something else getting clean.

Howson's Decree: you remember to mail a letter only when you're nowhere near a mailbox.

Hump's Law of Bicycling: the shortest route has the steepest hills.

Imram's Truism: if it isn't on the first page of Google, it doesn't exist.

Ingram's Hypothesis: a little ignorance can go a long way, generally in the direction of maximum harm.

Irk's Rumination: the crucial memo will be snared in the out-basket by the paper clip of the overlying correspondence and go to oblivion in file.

Jenner's Driving Code: there is no traffic until you need to make a right turn.

Jensen's Revelation: there are thirty-two points to the compass, meaning that there are thirty-two directions in which a spoon can squirt grapefruit; yet the juice almost invariably flies straight into the human eye.

Jensen's Corollary: in the event the squirt does not hit the eye, the spoon placed in the sink will position itself to maximise splash from the tap.

Kelley's Postulate: an executive will always return to work from lunch early if no one takes him.

Kitchen Rule: in a family recipe that you discovered in an old book, the most vital measurement will be illegible.

Lastra's Corollary: after an access cover has been secured by sixteen hold-down screws, it will be discovered that the gasket has been omitted.

Laura's Law: No child throws up in the bathroom. Ever.

Law of Ethics: kickbacks must always exceed bribes.

Law of Experience: it works better if you plug it in.

Law of Mathematics: if it's easy you are doing it wrong.

Lazy Rule: Can't reach it. Don't need it.

Lazy Rule 2: the farther away the remote is, the more you like what's already on TV.

Library Law: no matter which book you need, it's on the bottom shelf.

Life's Inference: whatever you want, you can't have; what you can have, you don't want.

Maah's Law: things firstly have to go right so they can go wrong.

Medical Law: pills to be taken in twos always come out of the bottle in threes.

Meskimen's Analysis: there's never time to do it right, but always time to do it over.

Murphy's Eighth Corollary: no matter what goes wrong, there's always someone who will say he knew it would.

Murphy's Law Amendment: one important fact about Murphy's Law was that it was not actually coined by Murphy, but by another man of the same name.

Murphy's Reprisal: any attempt to print Murphy's law will jam the printer.

Nature's Declaration: there's an unseen force which lets birds know when you've just washed your car.

Nelson's Proposition: the better the four-wheel drive, the further away you'll be when you get stuck.

Neville's Maxim: there's no special reason; it's just government policy.

Nurem's Note: the less you say the less you have to take back.

Ogden's Observation: you can't expect to hit the jackpot if your name is not in the hat.

Olsson's Observation: telling people "Don't go out and by up all the toilet paper" will cause people to go out and by up all the toilet paper.

Oxbourne's Corollary: if you explain it so clearly that nobody can misunderstand, somebody will.

Parental Proclamation: If they grow up to be doctors, take the credit. If they grow up to be lawyers, don't take the blame. If they become politicians, say they were switched at birth.

Parent Rule: if it tastes good, you can't have it; if it tastes awful, you must clean your plate.

Patient's Analysis: the more boring and out-of-date the magazines in the waiting room, the longer you will have to wait for your scheduled appointment.

Perkin's Rumination: love letters, business contracts and money due you always arrive three weeks late, whereas junk mail arrives the day it was sent.

Perseverance Postulate: perseverance is the hard work you do after you get tired of doing the hard work you already did.

Prince's Proposition: no matter where a man stands in the kitchen he's always in the way.

Punctuality Principle: the only things that start on time are those that you're late for.

Querry's Edict: Without that little voice in your head you wouldn't be able to read this. Hear it?

Queue Principle: the longer you wait in line, the greater the likelihood that you are in the wrong line.

Reece's Law: the speed of an oncoming vehicle is directly proportional to the length of the passing zone.

Repair Perversity : the more an item costs, the farther you have to send it for repairs.

Retrospective Ruling: no matter what it is, last year's was much better.

Rule of Driving Courtesy: if you allow someone to get in front of you, you both will have the same destination, and the other car will get the last parking space.

Samson's Inference: if you think the world is against you – it doesn't necessarily mean that it isn't.

Sander's Rumination: life is a game, the object of which is to discover the object of the game.

Sand's Discovery: laziness is the mother of nine inventions out of ten.

Search Proof: the first place to look for anything is the last place you would expect to find it.

Self Preservation Law: if your house is on fire, get out before tweeting about it.

Seminar Truism: No matter how late you are for the presentation there is always a vacant seat in the front row. And it's the only spare seat.

Snafu's Coincidence: the best investment opportunities are encountered when you are broke.

Surgeon's Ruling: never say "oops" while your patient is conscious.

Sustenance Paradox: for an organism's life to be continued another organism's life has to be discontinued.

Tax Law: the process by which money is collected from the people to pay the salaries of the men who do the collecting.

Teenager's Observation: they get hungry again even before the dishes have been washed.

The Heineken Uncertainty Principle: you can never be sure how many beers you had last night.

Thug's Effect: the bag that breaks is the one with the eggs.

Thurber's Axiom: the damage to anything rarely exceeds the excess premium paid.

Trader's Conclusion: if something's old and you're trying to sell it, it's obsolete; if you're trying to buy it, it's a collector's item.

Triviality Theorem: in a meeting the time spent on any item of the agenda will be in inverse proportion to the sum of money involved.

Watson' Law of Cleaning: if you start to clean the desk in the spare bedroom you will probably have to clean the garage to find what you need to finish cleaning the desk.

Wexton's Observation: on TV pure drivel tends to drive off ordinary drivel.

Wunner's Postulate: the less you enjoy serving on committees, the more likely you are to be pressed to do so.

Xavier's Annulment: many of the above laws may be bypassed by learning the simple art of doing without thinking.

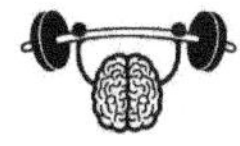

SUBTLE MORSELS
(Worth a second thought)

Two mates were out fishing in their tinnie and all they were catching were carp. One hooked a particular big one and, as he leaned over the side of the boat to net it, his wallet fell out of his top pocket. Before he could retrieve it, another carp swam by, grabbed the wallet and tossed it into the air. As it hit the water, another fish grabbed it and flicked it into the air as well.

This continued for several minutes, the wallet being flung from fish to fish.

His mate looked on in amazement and muttered, "Well bugger me. That's the first time I've seen carp-to-carp walleting."

~

A newly bereaved widow goes to the office of the local newspaper to place an obituary. As she is very short of money she asks for the minimum size announcement and hands over the message she would like.

It reads, "Harold dead. Funeral Thursday."

The editor takes pity on the old woman and points out she could have a few more words for the same money.

Thinking carefully the widow scribbled on the end, "Grey suit for sale. Worn once."

~

A real estate agent calls his friend, another agent, on the phone.

"Hey, how are you doing?" he asks.

"Well!" responds the friend. "I just sold a home for $1,800,000 this morning. I also have another sale certain to go ahead for $2 million. I have just got sole agency for a whole block of new apartments on the waterfront, and have had a record month in sales. How are you?"

"OK," says the first agent. "I'll call you back when you're alone."

Sarah, the self-appointed arbiter of the town's morals, stuck her nose into everyone's business. She made a mistake, however, when she accused her neighbour George of being an alcoholic after spotting his ute parked in front of a bar one afternoon.

"George, everyone who sees it there will know what you're doing," she told him in front of their church group.

George ignored her and walked away. Later that evening, he parked his ute in front of Sarah's house and left it there all night.

A Roman walks into a bar and asks for a martinus.

"You mean martini?" the bartender asks.

The Roman replies, "Slow down there. I'll let you know when I want more than one."

SUBTLE MORSELS
(Worth a second thought)

It's impossible to tiptoe around without activating your T-rex front arms.

And then Satan said, "Put the alphabet into maths."

Everybody says Wed-ens-day when writing Wednesday.

When you were a kid you sang the alphabet like A B C D E F G H I J K ELEMENO P? Why?

When you see lover's names carved in a tree don't you think it strange that so many people carry a knife on a date?

If they made footpaths wider the third friend would not have to walk behind and feel excluded.

Do not, under any circumstances, trust anyone who can bite into an ice cream without flinching. That is not natural.

He's as baffled as Adam on Mothers Day.

He's sharp as a cue ball, quick as a tree, and suffers from Clue Deficit Disorder.

If what you don't know can't hurt you, she's practically invulnerable.

Kites rise highest against the wind, not with it.

Be an optimist - it does not seem to be much use to be anything else. (Winston Churchill)

When the eagles are silent, the parrots begin to jabber.

I'm standing on the ashes of the person I used to be.

All these different shops are getting ridiculous, Toys R Us, Carpets R Us, Beds R Us. There's one near me that sells right-angled triangles - Pythag R Us.

If I'm not back in five minutes, just wait longer.

I would rather have questions that can't be answered than answers that can't be questioned. (Richard Feynman)

If smoking is so bad for you, why have I never met anybody who died from smoking?

Leftists are among the first to speak of their rights.

Home is where the bra isn't.

Let's do some of those "we shouldn't be doing this" things.

High heels take you closer to heaven, so why not?

Immorality is the morality of those who are having a better time.

If a genie grants you three wishes but says you cannot wish for more wishes, why not wish for more genies?

Any of you readers really good at stuff until people watch you do that stuff?

He was as subtle as a train wreck. On a boat.

I've grown to hate low ceilings.

I had a recurring dream once.

Some days you think you are surrounded by idiots. Other days you realise it is not some days.

Moses was the first person to use Control-C as a shortcut.

Do history exams get harder every year?

You have enemies? Good. That means you've stood up for something, sometime in your life. (Winston Churchill)

I changed my wi-fi password to 244466666 so when someone asks, I can say it is 123456.

Finally, after all these years, he got himself a sportscar. He split his eye open playing rugby.

Apparently, 3.5 out of 7 people overcomplicate things.

Some fashion designers obviously failed human anatomy exams.

There's a first time for everything except déjà vu.

With some people I meet, I feel sad for their dog.

So what happens to recycling bins when they're not needed?

The bartender said, "We don't serve time travellers here." A time traveller walks into a bar.

Has anyone else noticed the "brain" named itself?

Have no responsibility to live up to what others expect of you. That's their mistake, not your failing.

Contentment is the smother of invention.

You don't know what you didn't know until you know it.

A cube of cheese no larger than a die

May bait the trap to catch a nibbling mie.

Maths is the only place where people buy sixty watermelons and no one wonders why.

Never in the history of calming down has anyone calmed down after being told to calm down.

If you boil a funny bone it becomes laughing stock. That's humerus.

Freudian slips happen to the breast of us.

A geologist is just a fault finder.

Trust your gut. It knows what your head hasn't figured out yet.

Had trouble with physics in college. When I signed up I thought it said psychics.

Can you buy an entire chess set in a pawn shop? (Stephen Wright)

My sunglasses are prescription, so if they're stolen, it becomes two people who can't see.

If you're so caught up in avoiding lightning, you may not ever enjoy a single thunderstorm.

Feefiphobia is a chronic fear of giants.

The anti-aging ad that I'd like to see is a baby covered in cream, saying, "Ah! I've used too much!"

Lego is offensive to people with bad knees.

"As a matter of fact" is an expression that precedes many an expression that isn't.

You have to be odd to be number one.

The more ridiculous a belief system, the higher the probability of its success.

If a man who cannot count finds a four-leaf clover, is he still lucky?

The damn moon interfered with my view of the eclipse.

A circus freak of the future will be the incredible non-tattooed man!

Want tinsel? Place aluminium foil in the paper shredder.

For a year numbered 2020, it's amazing how blind some folks can be.

A state of bliss means having no idea what is really happening.

The rules were already broken when I got here.

Too much time on my hands. ┏(-_-)┛ ┗(-_-)┓ ┗(-_-)┛ ┏(-_-)┓

We'd like to give a shout out to all librarians ... Oops, we're sorry.

So this cowboy walks into a German car showroom and he says, "Audi!" (Tim Vine)

You begin cutting your wisdom teeth the first time you bite off more than you can chew.

"The leg, she is broken," he said in fractured English.

Answering your mobile when you do not recognise the number is like picking up a hitch hiker.

Historians are unsuccessful novelists.

Knowledge is realising that, while the street is one-way, wisdom is looking both directions anyway.

Contrary to popular belief, standing just a breath away from me does not make the line to the checkout any shorter.

A true friend is there for you when he'd rather be anywhere else.

People everywhere confuse what they read in newspapers with news.

Survivors of a plane crash in the wilderness must wonder how much their airport parking bill will be.

Buy the personalised number plate baa baa for your black jeep.

Nobody notices what you do, until you don't do it.

Not being able to sleep is a nightmare.

When a person tells you, "I'll think it over and let you know" - you know.

Ever wonder what "Please Do Not Touch" would be in Braille?

When anyone asks you, "What is it?", explain to them that "it" is a pronoun.

It takes one to know one - and vice versa.

No, I don't read. The letters get really repetitive after a while.

A line is a dot that went for a walk.

Try this. Go to beaches early in the morning and bury metal items with "Get a life!" written on them.

Don't insult the crocodile until you have crossed the river.

The road to success is often dotted with many tempting parking bays.

Some people create their own storms and then whinge when it rains.

Success is not forever and failure is never fatal.

Ever regret the many years you spent learning to write cursive?

A champion is someone who gets up when they can't.

If today were perfect there would be no need for tomorrow.

Bigotry is being certain of something you know nothing about.

One day go into a library and ask if they have any books on shelves.

When you truly love what you do, not working is hard work.

Bet you wish you could occasionally unmeet someone.

If you wish to hide your character, do not play golf.

Do all the things you think you could if you thought you would not fail.

Freedom of speech is unnecessary if the people to whom it is granted do not think for themselves.

Those who know the least want to be heard the most.

A lack of action is often mistaken for patience.

When New Zealanders emigrate to Australia, it raises the average IQ of both countries.

Why don't the post office get the Jehovah's Witnesses to deliver the mail on Saturday?

So I met an Egyptian - they walk just like us.

Education consists mainly of what we have unlearned. (Mark Twain)

We sold our vacuum cleaner because it was just gathering dust.

Talking louder does not make you any less wrong.

Nepotism: putting on heirs.

Madness takes its toll; please have exact change.

A hobby is hard work you wouldn't do for a boss.

Politeness is to society what oil is to a machine.

Those who fear the facts will forever try to discredit the fact-finders.

If you clean up you are depriving future archaeologists of clues to your daily life. Ever think about that?

When it comes to giving - some people stop at nothing.

Please keep me in your thoughts and prayers right now. Nothing is going on, I'm just a narcissist.

Do you know what you should be doing at 9 pm? Changing out of your day pyjamas and putting your night pyjamas on.

For a successful technology, reality must take precedence over public relations, for nature cannot be fooled. (Richard P Feynman)

Death is the number one killer in the world today.

A child will never spill anything on a dirty floor.

Moral indignation is jealousy with a halo. (HG Wells)

My favourite thing about camping is when I'm not.

Trying to do more is not as smart as having less to do.

Skinny jeans are easier to obtain than skinny genes.

I clapped because it was finished, not because I liked it.

Flattery is the sincerest form of lying.

The fly that does not want to be swatted is safest if it sits on the fly-swat.

Anyone who says you should question science does not understand that science is all about questioning.

Anyone who says the truth shall set you free has never been to traffic court.

If attacked by a mob of clowns - go for the juggler.

Be suspicious of all the things that the average citizen believes. (HL Mencken)

Life has no remote so get up and change it yourself.

You can move mountains by beginning to carry away small stones.

Givers have to learn limits because takers don't have any.

It can be better to cross the line than stand and just stare at the line for the rest of your life.

There are no short cuts to any place worth going.

Remember the seven deadly sins and have a great week.

Character is what you are in the dark.

The person who says "I may be wrong, but ... " does not believe there can be any such possibility. (Kin Hubbard)

Of all sad words of tongue or pen, the saddest is, "It might have been."

Your future self is watching you right now through memories.

There's no time to be bored in a world as beautiful as this.

Don't let yesterday take up too much of today. (Will Rogers)

If you misbehave and nobody sees you, that's one less lie you'll have to tell later.

If it doesn't challenge you it doesn't change you.

Stopping cyber bullying is simple - close your laptop.

Just because trouble comes visiting doesn't mean you have to offer it a place to sit down.

You gotta go for personality, guys, because they'll look like grandma someday.

We all do our best proofreading right after we hit "send".

When what you do speaks for itself, don't interrupt.

Opportunities always look bigger going than coming.

One of these days is none of these days.

Procrastination is opportunity's natural assassin.

I find that the further I go back, the better things were, whether they happened or not. (Mark Twain)

Everyone is conservative about what they know best.

Failure is an event, not a person. (Zig Ziglar)

You know all those things you've wanted to do? You should do them.

Cheer up! Remember the less you have, the more there is to get.

If you wish to die young, make your physician your heir.

History is the version of past events that people have decided to agree on. (Napoleon Bonaparte)

Their train of thought was derailed. There were no survivors.

Sometimes it is better to react with no reaction.

Try not to break the rules but by all means test their elasticity.

Never hate people who are jealous because they think you are better than them.

Just because nobody complains doesn't mean all parachutes are perfect.

We all know someone who just lacks the ability to realise that everyone in the room wants them to shut up.

My friend and I laugh about how competitive we are, but I laugh more.

What we learn after we know it all is what counts.

What you won't like about office Christmas parties is looking for a new job the next day.

Give me six hours to chop down a tree, and I will spend the first four hours sharpening the axe. (Abraham Lincoln)

You can melt a piece of ice just by staring at it. Might take a little longer than you initially thought.

One good thing about punctuality is that it's a sure way to help you enjoy a few minutes of privacy.

When a society has to resort to the lavatory for its humour, the writing is on the wall.

Tomorrow is often the busiest day of the week.

Our first daughter was born with a silver spoon in her mouth. Now we're hoping for triplets so we can have the whole set.

One of our team didn't show up for the pub quiz so we got a statistician to make up the numbers.

For as long as I remember I've had memories.

Five out of six people enjoy playing Russian Roulette.

If there's one thing I can't stand, it's tripods with one leg missing.

I think I speak for everyone when I say we hate being spoken for.

Chance favours the prepared mind. (Louis Pasteur)

Remember when we had to smack the TV because the channel wasn't coming in too clearly? I feel that way about far too many people.

People who are so ignorant that they use the wrong word should have the humidity to admit it.

People whose sliding glass or screen doors never come off their tracks, what do you do with the rest of your dark magic?

Don't do something permanently stupid just because you're temporarily upset.

Strive not to be a success only but rather be of value. (Albert Einstein)

If women ran the world we would not have wars; just intense negotiations every twenty-eight days.

The idea is to grow up by always finding opportunity in change.

Never die for your beliefs 'cos you might be wrong.

She was going to be a horologist, but then discovered it isn't what it sounds like.

Hermaphrodites are the only real single parents.

Learn from the mistakes made by people who took your advice.

Street human statues can also be made to move by taking money *out* of their hat.

The nicest feeling is to do a good deed anonymously and have someone find out about it.

A painting is worth a thousand confused art-gallery visitors.

To argue with a fool is like lighting candles for the blind.

A mute incontinent goes without saying.

What's the point of looking up the spelling of a word in the dictionary when you don't know how to spell it in the first place?

If you can't beat them, what's the point in becoming a teacher?

Why would they hang a whole jury just because they couldn't make up their minds?

The driver is safer when both the road and the driver are dry. (Brian Philipson)

When a mosquito lands on your testicles you realise there is always a way to solve a problem without violence.

Family reunions are when relatives gather from all over to be reminded why they scattered in the first place.

Congratulations! You just broke your record for most days lived.

In theory, there is no difference between theory and practice, but in practice, there is.

A group of owls is called a parliament, which is strange because owls are quite intelligent.

Change is good as long as nothing has to be done differently.

Why do we need algebra as finding X seems only useful if you're a pirate.

Vuja de: the feeling you've never been here.

Sometimes not getting what you want is a wonderful stroke of luck.

You never realise how much you swear until you are in a situation where you can't.

Saw an ad for burial plots and thought to myself: that's the last thing I need.

A friend is someone who listens attentively while you say nothing.

Well, if I can be of any help at all, you are in worse trouble than I thought.

This is interesting - toast is the only thing that can be eaten or drunk.

Scientists won't rest until they find a cure for insomnia.

It can be super hard to find a rap song on iTunes when you spell all the words correctly.

If you are coasting it probably means you are going down hill.

Carrots may be good for your eyes but booze doubles the vision.

Never needlessly disturb a thing at rest. Don't poke it.

Here's a joke for all you mind readers out there ...

Head of lettuce - that must be a boring job.

He knew he was going to fail his maths test when he entered the classroom, did a 360 and left.

Some people mistake their imagination for their memory.

To be or not to be. That's not really a question.

Seek to be worth knowing rather than well known.

Revenge is like biting the dog because the dog bit you.

Done is better than perfect.

Thursday the 12th is just as rare as Friday the 13th. (Neil deGrasse Tyson)

Instead of complaining that roses have thorns, rejoice in the fact that thorns have roses.

Just imagine for a moment a world without hypothetical situations.

Success usually comes to those who are too busy to be looking for it.

Creativity is a wild mind and a disciplined eye.

I'd rather have a life of "Oh, wells" than one of "What if's".

Do something today that your future self will thank you for.

A year from now you will wish you had started today.

If you change the way you look at things, the things you look at change. (Wayne Dyer)

My stupid *camera* won't stop ringing.

Wise people are not always silent but they know when to be.

"I" before "e" except after "c" is disproved by science.

I think I've seized the wrong bloody day.

Admire those who can give without remembering and take without forgetting.

People who try to bring you down are already below you.

Make it a Valentine's Day she'll always remember by simply forgetting it.

There is always a big temptation to settle for too little.

Take the chance while you still have the choice.

I know a lot of jokes about unemployed people but none of them work.

Just because you fail once doesn't mean you're gonna fail at everything. (Marilyn Monroe)

Yawning is your body's way of saying 20% of battery remaining.

A journey of two metres begins with a single, "Where the #%!= is the remote?"

No one has ever become poor by giving.

People who worry about tomorrow are always worried.

In disagreeing, it isn't necessary to be disagreeable.

The most important things in life aren't things.

Perfection is not attainable, but if we chase perfection we can catch excellence.

Even if they throw you to the wolves, return leading the pack.

If they gossip to you they'll gossip about you.

If you are willing to admit faults, you have one less fault to admit.

We are all guilty of all the good we did not do. (Voltaire)

Wisdom is knowing what to do with what you know.

Holding a grudge is letting someone live rent-free in your head.

BITE-SIZED BRIEFS

She met an amazing man at a party on Saturday. Wonderful listener, great looking ... She gave him her number and winked at him to call her when he got home. It's been four days. She's really starting to worry the poor guy is homeless.

Police officer approaches a woman on the beach. "I'm sorry, ma'am, but it's forbidden to bathe here."

The woman is surprised. "But why are you telling me now? You've just watched me put on my bikini and tanning oil?"

The police officer shrugs. "Well, that is not forbidden."

The police stop an old guy in questionable condition at 1 am. "What are you doing out so late, sir?" asks the police officer.

"I'm going to a seminar on 'The harmful effects of alcohol'," replies the man.

"Are you pulling my leg or something?!" says the police officer. "Who would hold a seminar like that at this hour?!"

The man sighs. "My wife."

A guy leans closer to his wife. "Can you keep a secret?" he whispers to her.

"Sure I can," says the wife, becoming curious.

"That's good," whispers the man again. "So can I."

Father looks at his teenage son. "James, you've been adopted."

James jumps up. "Adopted! I knew it! I want to meet my biological parents!"

Father laughs. "No, no, James, we are your biological parents. But you need to get packing. Your adoptive ones will be here in an hour."

A doctor tells a patient, "Sir, you are highly contagious and must be placed in isolation. Until we get in contact with the Centre for Disease Control and Prevention, your diet will consist of pizza and fried eggs."

"Will that help me get better again?" asks the patient.

"Not really. But it's the only thing we can shove in under the door."

An artist asked the gallery manager if anybody asked about his paintings.

"Well, there's good news and there's bad news," said the owner. "The good news is that a gentleman liked your work and asked if its value would appreciate after your death. When I said yes, he bought all twenty of your paintings."

"But that's fantastic," whooped the artist. "What could possibly be the bad news?"

"The gentleman was your doctor."

Give a man a fish and you will feed him for the day. Teach a man to fish and he's going spend a fortune on gear he'll only be using twice a year.

If 99.9% of all women find you unattractive, hang in there. You still have around forty million women who would find you attractive.

BITE-SIZED BRIEFS

"Brevity is the soul of wit," said Shakespeare in the play Hamlet.

That being so, these short one liners should provide you with some entertainment.

You didn't come this far to only come this far.

My brain has too many tabs open.

When two egotists meet it is an I for an I.

3.1415926 is a nice round number.

Dreams don't work unless you do.

Vacation calories don't count.

Spelling is my fortay.

Lawyers have feelings too, allegedly.

punctuation who needs it.

Life happens. Coffee helps.

Funny how inflammable things are flammable.

Smiles are always in fashion.

She was on cloud wine.

Pyromaniacs of the world, ignite.

Botox, it's not to be frowned upon.

Classical jazz is the rock of ages.

Action destroys procrastination. (Og Mandino)

Half of a large intestine = 1 semicolon.

Die young as late as possible.

Over analysis creates paralysis.

The favourite medical test result .... Benign.

Real Eyes. Realise. Real Lies.

A party without booze is just a meeting.

Quadruplets: four crying out loud.

Avoid clichés like the plague.

Criminal lawyer is a redundancy.

69 will never be a normal number.

If not now, when?

How do nudist clean their glasses?

Nothing works unless you do.

I'm proud of my humility.

The best antiques are old friends.

Honk if you love peace and quiet.

A friend in need is a pest.

Astronomy is looking up.

Let's have some new clichés.

Alexander the Average.

I'm a great lover, I'll bet.

Exactly how clean *is* a whistle?

Cleavage: the best popcorn catcher.

Sweat is just fat crying.

Echo one liners are a no no.

Death is hereditary.

Smart and witty beats fake and pretty.

Sock + Sandals = Beard.

Sixty years of age is only 16 Celsius.

Cut too many corners, you'll go in circles.

Luxury is being healthy.

Shit happens. Step over it.

Dentists call their X-rays tooth pics.

Five symptoms of laziness. 1.

Stop petting my peeves.

Minimalism is the new extra mile.

I'm smart enough to know that I'm dumb.

A punctual husband is a lonely man.

Living in a vacuum sucks.

Someday is not a day of the week.

You are not illiterate.

I don't sweat, she said, I sparkle.

A violinist is just a high-strung musician.

My fear of moving stairs is escalating.

Never try to out-stubborn a cat.

Texting isn't dating.

He's a recovering chocolate addict.

It's simple. If it jiggles, it's fat.

One in four frogs is a leap frog.

It's weird not to be weird.

Cats are entry-level demons.

To and too are two different words.

High heels are her arch enemy.

Before was was was, was was is.

Vacuuming sucks.

I never win at Scrable.

Graffiti-proof paint is unremarkable.

It's a short trip. While alive, live.

Impossible is for the unwilling.

Never regret anything that made you smile.

Don't bark if you can't bite.

Luck is the idol of the idle.

When in doubt, poke it with a stick.

I have a black belt in leather.

Debt doesn't buy happiness either.

There's no future in time travel.

Listening is silent flattery

You can't be late until you show up.

A dildo is the original selfie stick.

Fobia: the fear of misspelled words.

My apathy is at an all time whatever.

Let he without typos, cast the first store.

Zombies seem to enjoy long walks.

The future ain't what it used to be.

Believe you can and you're halfway there.

Only a thief wishes you prosperity in life!

Happy Monday is an oxymoron.

Don't abbrev.

Procrastinate now, don't put it off.

There's a lot to be said for mutes.

Cowards are very afraid to admit it.

Roundabouts are a revolutionary idea.

BIG SHOUT OUT to the partially deaf.

More confused than a cow on astroturf.

It's always too soon to quit!

Don't dwell, go higher.

It's unlucky to be superstitious.

Check this one out … 1.

An unemployed clown is nobody's fool.

If opportunity doesn't knock, build a door.

Life is funny. Well, yours is. To me.

Beware the hobby that eats.

Reuse, recycle, regift.

Survival rule: you go first.

Sadists are kind to a masochist.

So when is the next end of the world?

It should really be called "teethpaste".

He and his recliner go way back.

If it works, don't fix it.

Urinalysis: The study of pissed off people.

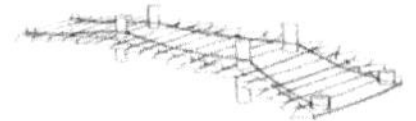

LONGER ONE LINERS
(Too good to leave out)

While some items are longer than the standard page width and might be termed "bastard" one liners, they are of such worth as to be included.

Of course we could fit them into one line with 9 point font size or smaller.

There are many short one liners, the shortest joke in the world being: "Pretentious? Moi?"

If short is your preference then the previous section may have satisfied you

GIVING AN ORANGE. When an ordinary man wants to give an orange to another, he simply says, "Here, have an orange."

When a lawyer does it, they say:

"Know all men by these present that I hereby give, grant, bargain, sell, release, convey, transfer and quit claim all my rights, title, interest, benefit and use whatever in, of and concerning this chattel, otherwise known as an orange, or *Citrus aurantium*, together with all of the appurtenances thereto of skin, pulp, pip, rind, seeds and juice, to have and to hold the said orange together with its skin, pulp, pip, rind, seeds and juice for his own use and behoof, to himself and his heirs, in fee simple forever, free from all liens, encumbrances, easements, limitations, restraints or conditions whatsoever, any and all prior deeds, transfers or other documents whatsoever, now or anywhere made to the contrary **not withstanding**, with full power to bite, cut, suck, or otherwise eat the said orange or to give away the same, with or without its skin, pulp, pip, rind, seeds or juice!"

And you think the future is going to get more complex?

An inter-office football game was held only once a year between the marketing and support staff of the company.

The support staff whipped the marketing department soundly.

To show just how the marketing department earns their keep with spin, they posted this memo on the bulletin board after the game:

"The Marketing Department is pleased to announce that for the 2021Season, we came in 2nd place, having lost but one game all year. The Support Department, however, had a rather dismal season, winning only one game."

The truck driver with his load of eight cars stacked on two levels of the trailer for delivery to dealers in North Queensland was halfway between two cities as the sun went down. As it got dark he switched on his truck's headlights, only to find that they were not working.

As with all long-haul drivers he was on a tight timetable for delivery of these new vehicles. He thought of a solution and pulled over, got up onto the front vehicle on the second level and switched on its headlights.

Worked well. He drove carefully, knowing on this stretch of more than one hundred kilometres between towns there were cattle and roos on the road he had to watch for.

Suddenly he saw an approaching car swerve off the road, across a ditch, through a fence and stopped up against a tree.

He pulled over, jumped out and went to see if he could help.

"What happened mate," he asked. "A roo or a mob of cattle across your path?"

"Nah," said the stunned driver. "It's just when I see headlights coming down the road towards me ten metres above the ground, I'm not going to hang around to see how wide the bastard is."

LONGER ONE LINERS
(Too good to leave out)

People who go for face lifts have a good idea that they are going to look younger after surgery, so why do they always look surprised?

In an argument over whether a glass was half empty or half full, just take the glass and put the contents into a smaller glass. Problem solved.

I don't think outside the box. I don't think inside the box. I don't even know where the hell the box is or even what a box is.

Ten million people in this world share the same birthday as you so your personalised horoscope means bugger all.

He learned a long time ago that there is something worse than missing the goal, and that's not pulling the trigger. Decide.

If you can only go left or right, and you know that left isn't right, then by a process of elimination, right must be right because it's the only way left. WTF?

My goal in 2021 is to accomplish the goals I set in 2020, which I should have done in 2019 because I made a promise in 2018, which I planned in 2013.

The people you care most about in life are taken from you too soon and all the less important ones just never go away.

Anti-conformists conform to the idea of not conforming and, if it were legal, anti-conformists would all drive on the road in reverse.

The factory of the future will have only two employees, a man, and a dog. The man will be there to feed the dog and the dog will be there to keep the man from touching the equipment.

He looked stupid walking around Woolworths when he took some advice recently and decided not to put all his eggs in one basket.

Instead of a blanket ban on smoking, the government should criminalise tobacco and legalise cannabis, then no one will care if anyone is smoking.

I don't want to sound like I'm bragging or anything, but if I make it to 2024, I will have survived my fifth "end of the world" prediction so far.

Life is like a Ferris wheel. One minute you're on the top, the next you are on the bottom. Just stay in your seat and hang on until you reach the top again.

Pessimists say that life is like holding your laundry and a sock falls, and when you go to pick it up, two more fall, and it finishes up with all the laundry on the floor.

When I met her I thought she was quiet. When she talked to me I wished she was quiet. Now when she is quiet I'm really scared.

That awkward moment when you take a shower late in the afternoon and have to decide whether to put on regular clothes or your pyjamas.

All horoscopes say the same thing - planets are doing stuff, so it's a good day to do stuff, but be prepared in case bad stuff happens.

The spread of the corona virus is based on two factors. 1) How dense the population is. 2) How dense the population is.

How do you approach the neighbours and tell them that their wi-fi isn't working properly and they might need to reset their modem?

Whenever they are condemning Botox or breast implants, some people speak so passionately that their false teeth almost fall out.

Apparently there's a correlation between the number of digits on a man's bank balance, and the number of things that his woman is willing to forgive him for.

Most employees don't really want to be highly paid; they just want to earn more than their peers, and, more importantly, more than their neighbours.

Twelve percent of people with glasses wear them as an attempt to see better while eighty-eight percent of people with glasses wear them as an attempt to appear smarter. Duh.

Life punishes those who have things in abundance by making them worry about petty things like what to wear, or which car to drive.

In my home town everybody knows what everybody else is doing, and all buy the weekly newspaper to see how much the editor dares to print.

Scientists say we use only 10% of our brain. Imagine how much better the world would be if we started using the other 60%.

In this age of technology, we learn something every day, and lots of times it's that what we learned the day before was wrong.

The correct way to punctuate a sentence that states: "Of course it is none of my business, but ..." is to place a period after the word "but".

We have long passed the Victorian era of writing when asterisks were followed after a certain interval by a baby. (Somerset Maugham)

Doing the same thing over and over again expecting different results isn't the definition of insanity (as said by Einstein), it's the definition of parenting.

No matter how stupid you feel, remember, Little Red Riding Hood couldn't figure out a talking wolf in drag wasn't her grandmother.

The older twin calls their little sibling fifty times a day and says, "When I was your age ..." and then describes what they did six minutes ago.

The Prime Minister says he'll put a cap on immigrants coming into the country. That's wrong. Immigrants should be allowed to wear what they like.

The farther away from the entrance that you have to park, the closer the space vacated by the car that pulls away as you walk up to the door.

I don't have a problem with idiots. I have a problem with the fact they have an internet connection. Where is the drone strike when you need one?

The Romans would never have found time to conquer the world if they had been obliged first to learn Latin. (Heinrich Heine)

It's not the way you look that reveals your age, rather it is your use of complete sentences, proper grammar and spelling when you text.

Yes I want to apply for your store credit card now, so let's go through the entire process now while the shoppers in line behind me fantasise about killing me.

A jury is a group of twelve people, who, having lied to the judge about their health, hearing, and business engagements, have failed to fool him.

You are well-bred if you wait in well-mannered silence while the loudmouth gets the service. Or else you are able to yawn with your mouth closed.

Damn, you suddenly realise that you're all grown up that moment when you actually pick up the ice cube instead of kicking it under the fridge.

Yet another robot lands on Mars and begins transmitting back photographs of rocks, thus confirming suspicions that the universe has a lot of rocks in it.

The idea of two people living together for more than twenty-five years without serious dispute suggests a lack of spirit only to be admired in sheep. (AP Herbert)

Your first job is to prepare the soil. The best tool for this is your neighbour's motorised garden tiller. If your neighbour does not own a garden tiller, suggest that he buy one.

Pain: an uncomfortable frame of mind that may have a physical basis in something that is being done to the body, or may be purely mental, caused by the good fortune of another. (Ambrose Bierce)

I just want to start by congratulating the previous speaker on their wonderful speech. I always knew it would be hard to follow and I was right. I couldn't follow a word of it.

If you need those extra hours on a Sunday morning, but the kids are being noisy? Just tell them, "OK, kids, wake me up in half an hour so we can finally get cracking on cleaning the house from top to bottom." You're welcome.

1998 - don't get in the car with strangers.
2008 - don't meet people from the internet alone.
2018 - UBER. Order a stranger from the internet and get into their car alone.

Don't you hate people who can go to sleep as soon as they shut their eyes. In my case it takes three hours, seven hundred position changes and a sacrifice to the gods.

If people are so amazed by crop circles, they should see the farm near my house. Aliens have somehow managed to cut down all the crops, roll them into enormous cylinder shapes, and stack them by the side of the field.

A pessimist sees only the dark side of the clouds, and mopes; a philosopher sees both sides, and shrugs; an optimist doesn't see the clouds at all - he's walking on them. (Leonard Levinson)

It may be time to start exercising because halfway up this flight of stairs and I'm considering setting up base camp and trying for the summit tomorrow.

I'm a passive-aggressive; that's what this counsellor labelled me, which really ticked me off, but I couldn't do a thing about it - not right then, but I have made plans. Just wait.

If you can't remember someone's name then ask them, "What was your name again?" Out of instinct, they tell you their first name. Then say, "Oh I knew that. I meant your last name!" And boom, you get the full name, and you're not rude. Clever!

Grandma learned that *Fifty Shades of Grey* was not a book about hair colour .

Is it true that ladies get more cleaning done in the ten minutes before someone comes over than they do in a normal week.

Men are strange. They have thirty-year mortgages, five-year car leases, two-year cell phone contracts and a lifetime gym membership, and then they say they're afraid of commitment.

Can anyone please tell me why, when a bird flies into a window, everyone feels bad for the bird, but when I walk into a sliding glass door, it's suddenly bloody hilarious?

Beauty isn't measured by outer appearance and what clothes we wear, but what we are inside. So, try going out naked tomorrow and bask in the admiration!

Your host's purpose in having a party is surely not for you to enjoy yourself; if that were their sole purpose they'd have simply sent champagne and women over to your place by taxi. (PJ O'Rourke)

Give a man a fish and he will eat for a day! Teach a man to fish and he will go out and purchase expensive fishing gear, stupid-looking clothes, a sports utility vehicle, travel one hundred kilometres to a lake, to stand waist high in water to catch two fish.

Isaac Newton had an apple fall on his head and has been labelled a genius for the last 350 years. I threw a banana out my car window and it hit a bloke on the head. Three hundred and fifty hours community service and a suspended sentence. How times have changed.

Have you ever seen a flock of geese flying in a V formation and wondered why one side is always longer than the other? It's because there are more geese on that side.

Are there are still undecided voters? Well, saw someone stare at the McDonald's menu for fifteen minutes before ordering just one cheeseburger with no cheese. So, yes, I do believe there are.

To frighten the current generation, put them in a room with a rotary phone, an analogue watch, a TV with no remote (add rabbit ears for fun) and leave instructions for use written in cursive.

Got a letter in the mail that read: "If you ever want to see you're wife alive again, leave $50,000 in unmarked bills in the waste paper bin on Chester St." Seriously, does no one know the difference between "your" and "you're" anymore?

It is a well-known fact that those people who want to rule people are, ipso facto, those least suited to do it ... Anyone who is capable of getting themselves made Prime Minister should on no account be allowed to do the job. (Douglas Adams)

Axiom: if, while you are in school, there is a shortage of qualified personnel in a particular field, then by the time you graduate with the necessary qualifications, that field's employment is glutted.

Married women are heavier than single women because single women go home, see what's in the fridge, and go to bed, while married women get home, see what's in the bed, and go to the fridge.

The maximum number of a particular fish that an angler can take in a day varies from place to place and species to species, but it is a largely theoretical restriction with little practical application.

Ever noticed that when there is a very long road upon which there is a one-way bridge placed at random, and there are only two cars on that road, it follows that: (1) the two cars are going in opposite directions, and (2) they will always meet at the bridge.

Karate is a form of martial arts in which people who have had years and years of training can, using only their hands and feet, make some of the worst movies in the history of the world. (Dave Barry)

Before the computer: Memory was something that you lost with age. An application was for employment. A program was a TV show. A cursor used profanity. A keyboard was a piano. A web was a spider's home. A virus was the flu.

The broccoli said it looked like a tree, the mushroom said it looked like an umbrella, the walnut said it looked like a brain and the banana asked to change the subject.

He lived in a house that ran on static electricity - if he wanted to run the blender, he had to rub balloons on his head; if he wanted to cook, he had to pull off a sweater really quickly. (Steven Wright)

When the biscuit I was dunking broke and sank to the bottom, I just sat there, staring at the cup and wondering why bad things happen to good people.

Going into a teenager's room is like going to Ikea. You pop in for a moment to take a look and come out with four bowls, six cups, a few plates and a set of cutlery.

Connoisseur: one who attains an obsessive knowledge of wines, audio equipment, cats or French cheeses so as to confer a sense of inadequacy on those who would simply enjoy them.

A telemarketer is a minimum-waged person who calls a bunch of people on a list to sell them something that they probably don’t need, and gets hung up on because the person being called usually has a mouth full of food.

He just spent $40 on a costume for his dog so he can win a work pet costume contest for a $10 coffee gift card. Does he regret it? Nope. Karen from accounting and her cat are going down.

Impossible Lie: in golf, a ball that is in a position that is both completely obstructed by an immovable object and continuously observed by an incorruptible player.

Ninety-eight percent of the adults in this country are decent, hardworking, honest Australians. It's the other lousy two percent that get all the publicity; but then, we elected them.

Martial Arts: a family of Asiatic self-defence disciplines consisting largely of sweeping ornamental gestures of the arms and legs - amusing to look at but disappointingly ineffective when one's opponent is armed with a semi-automatic weapon.

Next time you ride on a roller coaster, take some spare bolts with you and just as it starts to move, tap the person in front of you and say, "These just fell out of your seat."

The average time between throwing something away and needing it badly is two weeks. This time can be reduced to one week by retaining the thing for a long, long time first.

It is invariably true that after the last of sixteen mounting screws has been removed from an access cover, it will be discovered that the wrong access cover has been removed.

Can anyone explain why no matter how many rooms there are in the motel, the fellow who starts up his car at five o'clock in the morning is always parked under your window?

Before you take your road trip, remember the probability of getting lost is directly proportional to the number of times the direction-giver says, "You can't miss it."

Group therapy is really just drama-in-the-round staged for the entertainment of a professional therapist, who commands the players to put on a new show each week and charges them for the privilege.

The best way to garden is to put on a wide-brimmed straw hat and some old clothes. And, with a hoe in one hand and a cold drink in the other, tell somebody else where to dig.

We would have discovered the cure for cancer by now if we rewarded, recognised and respected our scientists just as much as we do our sportsmen and celebrities.

W T F?

The judge explained to the female witness that the jury must have knowledge of exactly what was said by the defendant when he allegedly accosted and abused her with the most lurid, foul and insulting sexual suggestions imaginable.

The witness said it was so vile she could not possibly repeat what was said.

The judge insisted that the jury must know exactly what was said and finally asked the witness if she was prepared to write it down. She agreed and wrote it in a note.

The note was passed around the jury with looks of dismay and disgust as they read it. The lady juror nudged her neighbour juror who had been dozing during the proceedings and handed him the note.

He read it, read it again, smiled at her, nodded and put the note in his pocket.

A little old lady wrote to the state manager of Telstra, complaining strenuously about the foul language being used by two linesmen working outside her home.

The state manager called for a full report of the incident from the men involved and the memo he received was ...

Dear sir,

Me and Harry were working up the poles outside this lady's home. Harry was working above me with a tin of molten lead doing some repairs.

He spilt some of the red hot lead down the back of my shirt and I said, "Really Harry, you'll have to be more careful in the future."

Following the pandemic, universities are offering a new list of short programs to generate much needed income. New certificate level qualifications are offered in the following:

Elective Surgery in the Home

Prolonging Creative Suffering

The Joys of Hypochondria

How to Profit from Your Own Body

Achieving Guilt Without Sex

Under-Achievers Guide to Very Small Business

Sinus Drainage at Home

Ego Gratification Through Violence

Post-Coital Rug Making

High Fibre Sex (Theory and Practice)

Tap Dancing Your Way to Ridicule

Cultivating Viruses in Your Refrigerator

How to Make $500 in Real Estate

Burglar-Proofing Your Home with Concrete

Career Opportunities In Algeria

How to Tell an Orgasm from a Heart Attack

Vasectomy Reversal Using Kitchen Utensils

The Remote Control—overcoming your dependency

Novice to Abbot: "Can I smoke while I pray?"

"Certainly not!"

Later: "Can I pray while I smoke?"

"Go right ahead, my son".

My wife's seen some of the big Christmas presents I've been wrapping, and she looked at the one with her name on it and said, "Darling, a surfboard! You know I love the beach."

She might be even more excited when she sees the legs that are meant to go under it that I had to wrap separately.

Yet, for thousands of years even the calendar has recognized WTF with Wednesday, Thursday, Friday.

W T F?

When you get a call from a telemarketer, whisper, "It's done but there is blood everywhere."

Do you often find yourselves questioning a question with a question when questioned?

Why is it that when you pay someone a compliment they proceed to list their faults with, "Yes but ..."

I am not such a bad person ... After all, have you ever met anybody I murdered?

Road courtesy: dim unto others as you would have them dim unto you.

All right, who left the bag of idiots open?

Neil Armstrong lands on the moon: five pictures. Girl goes to Starbucks: forty-seven pictures.

There is no exception to the rule that every rule has an exception. (James Thurber)

Freedom of the Press means freedom to print such of the proprietor's prejudices as advertisers don't object to.

Celebrities are people who are well known for their well-knownness.

A circle, a rhombus, a pentagon and a scalene triangle walk into a bar. The rhombus says to the circle, "Your round"'

If you think the world is getting more unsafe, violent and unpredictable, the thirteenth century would like a word with you.

A power-generating windmill will fall apart before generating as much energy as it took to build it.

Thanks, autocorrect. I'm sure she's dying to know about my huge peninsula.

If only I could grow green stuff in my garden like I can in my refrigerator.

When your partner wants to have intercourse, pull up a chair and start talking.

There are some days when even my lucky underpants cannot help.

He was so lazy, if he had a third hand, he'd need a third pocket to put it in.

Boy, those French. They have a different word for everything. (Steve Martin)

Trouble knocked at the door, but, hearing laughter, hurried away.

Giraffes can lick their own ears.

Why do we have to pronounce record and record differently, as it is with live and live; and why does "gigantic" have two different sounding g's?

Nine out of ten Australians believe that out of ten people, one person will always disagree with the other nine.

When at school he belonged to a band called the Happy Funk Band but, due to a typo, they were expelled.

The silkworm moth has eleven brains.

Most cockatoos are left handed.

The Icelandic Parliament is the oldest surviving parliament in the world. It was founded in 930 AD.

Although the Great Fire destroyed much of London, only six people died.

Flies take off backwards.

Graduation speech: I would like to thank Wikipedia, and the copy/paste function.

The ballpoint pen was invented by the Biro brothers.

Mickey Mouse was originally called Mortimer.

I hope you go before me because I don't want you singing at my funeral. (Spike Milligan)

Some people at the self-checkout look like they are trying to operate a nuclear reactor.

Oh dear, just realised that I'm still "it" from a game of tiggy in 1987.

Ever spent minutes in the car looking for your phone, while using your phone as a flashlight?

The pet shop had a sign saying "For Sale, Chameleon" next to an empty cage. Hmmmm.

When an American says, "You do the math," you should also offer to assist them with their grammar.

A clairvoyant is a person who has the power of seeing that which is invisible to her patron, namely, that he is a dopey bastard.

Half a dozen because saying "six" is way too long.

Recent studies show that there were some studies done recently.

Did you know, the average person has one fallopian tube?

The louder he talked of his honesty and integrity, the faster we counted our spoons.

Everyone seems normal until you get to know them.

Waking up late is a great way to see which steps of your personal hygiene are really unnecessary.

There's nothing sadder than the look on a dog's face after he hears something hit the floor and discovers it's only lettuce.

April Fools' Day is the worst day ever to have a heart attack.

No word in the English language rhymes with month, orange, silver, or purple.

Be yourself, everyone else is taken. (Oscar Wilde)

After adding two weeks to the schedule for unexpected delays, add two more for the unexpected, unexpected delays.

If you spend your day in a well, can you say that your day was well-spent?

It's amazing how much trouble you can get into if you have nothing to do.

To cut a long story short, use fewer words.

May you live so long that no one wants to see you naked.

Dear optimist, pessimist and realist, while you were arguing about how full the glass of water was, I drank it. Sincerely, The opportunist.

If the boy was any dumber he'd have to be watered twice a week.

If you didn't want me knocking it over, why the hell did you write "tip jar" on it?

The new Superman movie is just two hours of Clark Kent frantically searching for a phone box

"It's not you, it's me." - Twins going through a photo album.

Warning: as soon as you're doing what you wanted to be doing, you want to be doing something else.

The world record for enjoying jazz is forty-eight seconds.

Will Will will the will to Will?

Seat belts are not as confining as wheelchairs.

The word "queueing" has five consecutive vowels. Who knew?

The inventor of pseudonyms is unknown.

I don't see the point in decimals.

A boomerang that does not come back is called a stick.

Saw a sign in a shop window, "We treat you like family." No way am I going in there.

A celebrity is one who is known to many persons he is glad he doesn't know. (HL Mencken)

For sale: Braille dictionary. Must see to appreciate.

The inventor of the time machine has tragically died in a car crash, next week.

His sister's expecting a baby, and he doesn't know if he's going to be an uncle or an aunt.

To reduce your carbon footprint take bigger steps.

I don't believe in reincarnation and I didn't believe in it when I was a rabbit.

I asked Alexa what women want and she hasn't shut up for six days.

We've heard that ignorance of maths is growing geometrically, whatever that means.

Ever think that when you step on the brakes, your life is in your foot's hands?

Needs a speed bump between his brain and his mouth.

I'm never included in anything, so I know how batteries feel.

There are those who give 110%, and those who passed fourth-grade maths.

Pretend to be a skilled pharmacist by taking half an hour to put some tablets in a bag.

You can be in therapy to learn how to deal with people who should be in therapy.

Shit. Why do clothes pockets only get caught on door handles when you are in a bad mood?

I went to Woolies to buy shampoo. Spent $150 and forgot the shampoo. Sound familiar?

May the mass x acceleration be with you.

Well, another day has passed and I did not use algebra once.

When you place a call that is being recorded for quality assurance and training purposes, make sure to say F%#&@er a lot.

My entire life can be summed up in one sentence: "Well that bloody well didn't go as planned."

Please note in this library the books in the post-apocalyptical fiction section have been moved to current affairs.

Some complain that there is nothing left to complain about.

People who stutter seem less different or more confident in winter.

She rolled her eyes so hard she saw her brain.

Her house-keeping style is best described as: "There appears to have been a struggle."

To see all pessimists as pessimists is to be a pessimist.

Nothing is more irritating than not being invited to a party you wouldn't be seen dead at.

"My name is immaterial," she said. "That's a pretty name," he replied.

Use three gallons of water to rinse out the yogurt container so it can go into the recycling bin.

The response to "Do you mind if I smoke?" is "I don't care if you burn."

Seventy-nine percent of accidents happen in the home so that's good news for the homeless.

WTF? New mouthwash says "24 Hour Protection ... use twice daily."

What does the word for dots looks like in Braille?

If you are talking to me and I appear as if I'm attentively listening, I'm probably just silently correcting your grammar in my head.

Invented a wireless, battery-free, hand-operated hair dryer - a towel.

Why did he put a wheelbarrow in his shopping cart at Bunnings?

You can't make everyone happy. You're not an avocado.

Oops! No, I meant he has the brains of a horse and is hung like Einstein.

Axiom: the fatter the man, the more Hawaiian the shirt.

The guy at the urinal next to me is now rethinking his decision to wear thongs today.

If you can fold a fitted sheet, you're obviously a witch.

People with halitosis are far and away the best.

If I go and visit a plastic surgeon, will he let me pick my nose?

Spoiler Alert: Siamese cats are just one cat, not two cats in one.

Every so often, I try to fornicate a large word into conversation, even if I'm not sure what it means.

Me? An egotist? Of course I'm an organ donor. Who wouldn't want a piece of this?

The rotation of Earth really makes my day.

They are so skinny they'd have to stand up twice to make a shadow.

Old MacDonald was dyslexic IEIEO. (Billy Connolly)

Do you follow where I'm coming from?

Seat belts are for kids: Hug them at home. Belt them in the car.

He was as important as a white crayon.

Million-to-one chances crop up nine times out of ten.

To the makers of rice cakes; thanks for nothing.

Most pirates get their eye patches just a little while after they get their hooks.

Had a great day. Got so much procrastinating done.

To everyone who received a book from me last Christmas, they are due back at the library next Friday.

Art is anything you can get away with.

You've been eating hot dogs and other fast foods for years but won't get the COVID vaccine because "you don't know what's in it?"!

A boomerang is just a frisbee for people who don't have any friends.

All of us could take a lesson from the weather. It pays no attention to criticism.

If you go through two lighters a day you are a heavy smoker.

Wonder what Captain Hook's name was before he lost his hand.

He never seemed to be doing anything, and yet he did not like to be disturbed at it.

Today's newspapers are only half the size they used to be because previously they would print both sides of the story.

Note there is only one letter difference between here and there. So?

His first mistake was thinking she couldn't hit a moving target.

Camera lenses are round, so why are photos square?

Ever notice that it sometimes takes a full eight hours to get nothing done?

Try to think how you can think about what you want to think.

A polygamist's life won't be complete until he finds that special somefive.

We'll have less of that, a bit more often.

The first rule for those with a bad memory: 1)

CAUTION: reading the entire medication warning may cause drowsi ...

He travels fastest who travels alone, but he hasn't anything to do when he gets there.

Are you tired of boiling water every time you make pasta? Boil a few gallons at the beginning of the week and freeze it for later.

All things being equal, all things are never equal.

Careful buying a watch if it says you can swim with it. This only applies if you can already swim without it.

Film *may* contain nudity? Either it does or it doesn't - don't waste my time.

Where are the calculations that go with the calculated risk?

If you haven't tried blind-folded archery you don't know what you're missing.

I was voted most likely to travel back in time by the class of 2047.

I don’t believe in astrology; I’m a Sagittarius and we’re sceptical. (Arthur C Clarke)

Ever misjudged how much shopping you wanted to buy and still not gone back to get a basket?

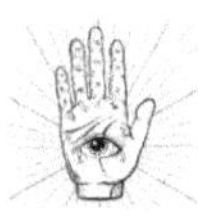

FELL OFF A TRUCK
(A mishmash medley of leftovers)

A blonde was down on her luck. In order to raise some money, she decided to kidnap a kid and hold him for ransom. She went to the playground, grabbed a kid, took him behind a tree, and told him, "I've kidnapped you."

She then wrote a note saying, "I've kidnapped your kid. Tomorrow morning, put $10,000 in a paper bag and put it under the fig tree next to the slide on the north side of the playground." Signed, Blonde.

The blonde then taped the note to the kid's shirt and sent him home to show it to his parents. The next morning the blonde checked, and, sure enough, a paper bag was sitting beneath the fig tree.

The blonde opened the bag and found the $10,000 with a note that said, "How could you do this to a fellow blonde?"

~

The waitress ignores him.

The man politely asks again, "Can you let me know about the menu please."

The waitress ignores him again.

The man, being the gentleman he was, asks again, "I want to know the menu please!"

The waitress gets very irritated and responds, "It's none of your damn business to know about the men I please."

~

An industrial chemist walks into a pharmacy and asks the pharmacist, "Do you have any sodium salt of acetylsalicylic acid?"

"You mean aspirin?" asked the pharmacist.

"That's it. I can never remember that word."

~

Her newly retired husband was watching as she went about her daily routine. She vacuumed, cleaned, ironed and sorted the laundry, and, after making them both a cup of coffee, she sat down.

Hubby looked at her thoughtfully. Was he finally realising he could help, she wondered?

Her hopes were dashed when he said, "Isn't it wonderful how you always find ways to keep yourself so busy."

~

In a couple's home, trying to fix their internet connection, the husband called out to his wife in the other room for the computer password.

"Start with a capital S, then 123," she shouted back.

He tried "S123" several times, but it didn't work. So he called the wife in.

As she input the password, she muttered, "I really don't see what's so difficult about typing Start123."

~

A waiter asked the customers what they wanted to drink. "Tea or coffee, gentlemen?"

The first man said, "I'll have tea."

The second man answered, "Me, too - and be sure the glass is clean!"

The waiter nodded and went off to the kitchen. He returned quickly, holding a tray with two cups.

He looked at the customers and said, "Two teas. Which of you two gentlemen asked for the clean glass?"

A little eight-year-old girl asks her mother, "Mum, what does virgin mean?"

Mum has been preparing for this moment for almost a year, recognising that her daughter was getting to that age when she would have been talking to her young friends at school, and was aware that today's children were far more aware than she was at that age.

Mum had prepared herself well for "the talk" and had decided that the best approach was to be specific and biological rather than use the birds and the bees approach.

After five minutes of detailed discussion covering all aspects of human reproduction she was pleased the moment had come and gone quite successfully. She then asked the young girl why she had enquired.

The daughter answered, "Well, it says here on the bottle, 'Virgin Olive Oil'. So what were you talking about, Mum?"

FELL OFF A TRUCK
(A mishmash medley of leftovers)

If it weren’t for Mondays, we’d all hate Tuesdays.

Some people couldn't be nice even if a unicorn waved a fairy wand over them while Judy Garland sang "Somewhere over the Rainbow".

A broad smile is a cooler way of showing your enemies that you have teeth.

I’m never late. The others are simply too early!

Einstein developed a theory about space and it was about time, too!

Writing my name in cursive is my signature move.

Even duct tape can't fix foolishness, but it can muffle the sound.

If you're bad at haggling, you'll end up paying the price.

Quantity is what you count; quality is what you count on.

There are people who are living proof that total brain failure does not always lead to physical death.

It is often said that before you die your life passes before your eyes. It is in fact true. It's called living.

Whether you’re first or last in the queue depends which way you're looking.

Life is like a ten-speed bike: most of us have gears we never use.

I am currently unsupervised. I know, it freaks me out too but the possibilities are endless.

Practice does not make perfect. Practice makes permanent. Only perfect practice makes perfect.

A signature always reveals a man's character - and sometimes even his name.

Cast your bread upon the waters but make sure the tide is coming in.

A person's character may be learned from the adjectives which they habitually use in conversation.

Action speaks louder than words but not nearly as often.

Good friends, good books and a sleepy conscience. This is the ideal life.

Let us be thankful for the fools. But for them, the rest of us could not succeed.

The man with a new idea is a crank until the idea succeeds.

I don't regret burning my bridges, but I do regret that there were not some people on them when I did.

It's easier to suffer in silence if you're positive someone is watching.

A small ATM room having two power outlets and eight downlights working 24 hours is asking me not to print a receipt to save the environment. Bull shit.

What can be asserted without evidence can also be dismissed without evidence.

People tell me I take mini-golf too seriously, but my caddy disagrees.

Gossip is hearing something you like about someone you don't.

If idiots could fly this would be an airport.

If your car breaks down near a Dominos order a pizza to be delivered and get a lift with the driver. Glad to be of assistance.

The only thing worse than the one that got away is the one that won't go away.

Don't question authority. It doesn't have a clue.

Gossip is the art of saying nothing in a way that leaves practically nothing unsaid.

I usually get my stuff from people who promised somebody else that they would keep it a secret. (Walter Winchell)

Gossip is anything that goes in one ear and over the back fence.

Pessimist sees darkness, optimist sees light, realist sees light and the coming train. Train driver sees three idiots sitting on the rails.

Sometimes the thoughts in my head get so bored they go out for a stroll through my mouth.

The first five days after the weekend can be boring.

It's not that I believe that there are too many idiots in this world, just that lightning is not distributed right. (Mark Twain)

His problem was not knowing he is the problem.

Have you ever said "what" three times, still do not know what was said, so you just agree?

I took the road less travelled and now have no idea where I am.

It has been so dry this month, the trees are whistling for the dogs.

Today's mighty oak is just yesterday's nut that held its ground.

Having lost sight of his objective he redoubled his efforts.

Wearing a black shirt renders soy stains invisible.

Mark my words, I collect highlighters.

My conscience is clean - I have never used it.

When girls have a great night out, they talk about it for months, but when blokes have a great night out, that night will never be spoken of.

Sign for a lounge furniture store. "Shack of Sit."

You can always tell when a person's well-informed. Their views are pretty much like yours.

Just how childlike golf players have become is proven by their frequent inability to count past five.

Don't worry about biting off more than you can chew; your mouth is probably a whole lot bigger than you think.

Why lower my standards to accommodate those who refuse to raise theirs?

I need professional help. A chef, a sommelier, a butler, a maid and a gardener will do just fine.

Diplomacy is the ability to do and say the nastiest thing in the nicest way.

Benefit of procrastination is that you always have something planned for tomorrow.

Good things come to those who wait, but they are the leftovers from those who hustle.

She is a peacock in everything but beauty. (Oscar Wilde)

There is nothing louder than a party across the street that you weren't invited to.

There is this golfer who cheated so badly that he once had a hole in one and wrote down zero on his scorecard.

I went window shopping yesterday and bought four windows. (Tommy Cooper)

Mosquito: an insect that makes you like flies better.

If you live to be a hundred you've got it made. Statistics show that very few people die past that age.

If you ever see her running, run like hell too because she's far too lazy to be running without a good reason.

Meanwhile, in a parallel universe: "Oh for God's sake! Where are all these extra single socks coming from?"

There is always one person at the card table who has to be told it is their turn.

When she starts "first of all "in the middle of an argument, just give up. She has won already as she is going to bring up stuff from ten years back.

Half the time people hug you they are just wiping their hands on your back.

A night of insomnia is usually followed by a morning of browser history clearing.

A diplomat is one who thinks twice before saying nothing.

All the world is mad save for me and thee, and sometimes I wonder about thee.

Would the person who took the step ladder yesterday please bring it back or further steps will be taken.

The farmer allows walkers to cross the field for free, but the bull charges.

Busier than a one-legged man in a arse kicking contest.

Well, enough about me. Let’s talk about you. What do you think about me?

Remember the age when sitting "boy girl boy girl" used to be a punishment?

Some people will not admit their faults. I would if I had any.

Anybody can grow older. That doesn't take any talent or ability.

He was so up himself he was like the rooster which thought the sun rose to hear it crow.

Few things are harder to put up with than the annoyance of a good example.

If you see someone wearing camouflage walk right into them so they know it's working.

My education was dismal. I went to a series of schools for mentally disturbed teachers. (Woody Allen)

More than 99% of facts are not and will never be useful to even a single person.

It's times like these, when I'm seated in bed with my computer on my knee, that I really wish I'd bought a laptop.

The only thing you can believe in newspapers is the date.

A man between two lawyers is like a fish between two cats.

After you've read three different reviews of the same film, you start to wonder about history.

If at first you don't succeed, find out if the loser gets anything.

If it wasn't for John Logie Baird, the inventor of television, we'd all still be eating frozen radio dinners. (Johnny Carson)

Anybody who says they could never conceive of killing another human being just needs to meet more people.

Guess what, YouTube, I will always, "Skip this ad," so why persist with it?

He looked as though he'd been weaned on a lemon.

Promises, really large promises, are the soul of advertising.

Remember when there were no wheels on suitcases and we carried them wherever we went?

It's hard to lead a cavalry charge if you think you look funny on a horse.

It takes less time to do a thing right than it does to explain why you did it wrong.

Me lazy? Nope, just in energy-saving mode.

People who are crazy enough to think they can change the world are the ones who do.

If you retain nothing else, always remember the most important Rule of Beauty, which is: "Who cares?"

Friends say I always contradict them, but I disagree.

She was so good at sleeping she could do it with her eyes closed.

Some drink at the fountain of knowledge. Others just gargle.

Getting information off the Internet is like taking a drink from a fire hydrant.

The surprising thing about young fools is how many survive to become old fools.

His pooled emotions wouldn't fill a teaspoon. (Dorothy Parker)

If you've got it, flaunt it. If you ain't, fake it.

Always look for the fool in the deal. If you don't find one, it's you.

If everything seems under control, you're just not going fast enough.

They say nothing is impossible, but I do nothing every day.

Thing about the law is that one size fits all.

So many big words. Such a small dictionary.

Put your big boy pants on and stop squealing.

Not unlike a long walk in tight shoes.

Does anyone else's day start backwards by waking up tired and going to bed wide awake?

Changing the toilet paper roll will not cause brain damage.

The brain has around one hundred billion neurones in it. Makes you think doesn't it?

The problem with temptation is that you may not get another chance.

Life is like underwear - change is good.

The best way to cheer yourself is to try to cheer someone else up. (Mark Twain)

Doing nothing is very hard; you never know when you're finished.

People who never do any more than they get paid for, never get paid for any more than they do. (Elbert Hubbard)

To know how important you think you are, you should do what you learned in kindergarten; be patient and wait your turn.

Who knew that "Wet Floor" signs are not a request?

If laziness was an Olympic sport, he said he would want to come in fourth so he wouldn't have to walk up to the podium.

A cricket match is twice as much fun if you're seeing it on the company's time.

Somewhere, something incredible is waiting to be known. (Carl Sagan)

The two most important days in your life are the day you're born and the day you find out why. (Mark Twain)

Physical scars last forever; mental scars only while you're sober.

First Olympic sailing result just in. GB have taken gold, Australia have taken silver and Somalia have taken the boat.

It's always funny until it happens to you.

I always know the right thing to say, immediately after the right time to say it has passed.

A lot of problems would disappear if people talked to each other more than talking about each other.

Say no to drugs and socks with sandals.

Birds don't sing, they're just screaming because they're scared of heights.

"I don't mean to brag" is something people say right before they brag.

Touching a surface that is unexpectedly wet with some unknown liquid can be extremely unnerving.

Who is ever emotionally ready for tomorrow to be Monday?

Sleep well, middle finger, you have a big day ahead of you tomorrow.

Surely thinking positive will attract negative things? It's basic physics.

Don't give a woman advice; one should never give a woman anything she can't wear in the evening. (Oscar Wilde)

Some people need to appreciate the effort I put into not being a serial killer.

Some people walked into my life and made it better. Others walked out and made it fantastic.

I know around 190% of the topics for my maths exam next week but, unfortunately, percentages isn't one of them.

Some things are best left unsaid, which I realise just after I've said them.

Sarcasm is the ability to insult idiots without them realising it.

The fact that no one understands you does not mean you are an artist.

Be smart because you won't be pretty forever.

Anyone who has time to clean is not spending anywhere near enough time reading.

"Your Honour, weed is not a drug, it's a plant. Therefore, I am not a dealer, I'm a florist."

Lying in advertising: deodorant scent that contains the words "active" or "sport" in its name.

Throwing in the towel only means more laundry. Don't do it.

I'm a leader not a follower. Unless it's dark or there is a spider in the room, then you go first.

Old school. You wake up with your eyebrows already on your face.

We swear because sometimes, "Gosh darn" and "Gee whiz" don't seem to work.

Early to bed, early to rise makes people suspicious.

When you don't know what you are doing, it's best to do it quickly.

God grant me the serenity to accept the terms and conditions I will not read.

Judging by all the cracking and popping noises my body makes when I work out, I'd say I'm about 74% Rice Bubbles.

Don't sign anything without pretending to read it first.

I'm not arrogant. I just don't like you.

Putting the fun into dysfunctional.

One needs to reassess one's life if one has more clothes to sleep in than to go out in.

Your secrets are safe with me. I wasn't even listening.

Made a huge to-do list today and just need to figure out who's going to do it.

If hard times make you stronger then I should be able to beat Superman up by now.

Some things are best said with an eye roll.

Who knew rock bottom was so crowded?

A social-justice warrior is a man who punches you in the face then whines that you bruised his fist.

Ever cleaned out your car and found seven half-empty water bottles?

Wouldn't you like to make it through one entire day without a single WTF moment?

Worrying about the future is a thing of the past.

To get through life, laugh your way through it. You either have to laugh or cry, so laugh because crying will give you a headache.

I don't like morning people, or mornings, or people.

Most people hate Mondays, Tuesdays, Wednesdays, Thursdays, and half of Fridays.

There is a door made entirely from seeds that opens by voice command: "Open Sesame."

The path to inner peace begins with four words: "Not my bloody problem."

All socks should be sold in packs of three as a precaution against losing one.

Surely memory foam mattresses should remind you what her name is.

A genius is one who can do anything except make a living.

A genius is one who shoots at something no one else can see - and hits it.

We hate to have some people give us advice because we know how badly they need it themselves.

Having no opinion is not enough; you also have to be incapable of expressing it. Please.

A learning experience is one of those things that says, "You know that thing you just did? Don't do that."

There never has been nor ever will be a sunrise so beautiful that it is worth waking me up to see it.

You never run out of things that can go wrong.

Tuesday is Monday's ugly sister.

Historical fact: until they invented the other side of Velcro, it never caught on.

The trouble with trouble is it starts out as fun.

Of course your opinion matters; just not to me.

An editor of a newspaper is someone who has to separate the wheat from the chaff and then print the chaff.

Hear no evil and speak no evil and you'll never be invited to a party. (Oscar Wilde)

People generally see what they look for and hear what they listen for.

It is not necessary to react to everything you notice. You have a right not to care.

Ever notice how ignorance picks up confidence as it goes along?

Laughing helps. It's like jogging on the inside.

The main trouble with mental notes is the ink fades so fast.

Remember when yoga was called Twister?

Aerobics comes from two Greek words: "aero", meaning "ability to", and "bic", meaning to "withstand extreme boredom".

We don't ever use that room because there was a spider in it once.

If you are offended by the things I say, imagine the stuff I hold back.

Always play fairly when you have the winning cards.

Getting one's knickers in a knot achieves nothing except making you walk funny.

Be careful. If a person is smiling all the time they are probably selling something that does not work. TV advertorials, I have you in mind.

On the rare occasions I seem to have all the ducks in a row the bloody things waddle off in all directions.

At the end of the day, life should ask us if we want to save the changes.

If you think things can't get worse it's probably only because you lack sufficient imagination.

When you are feeling sad, just remember that somewhere in the world some fat kid has just dropped his favourite ice cream.

Gossiping is just sharing opinions about other people's life choices.

Some people give my middle finger an erection.

When you misplace something and they ask, "Where did you have it last?" don't they know what misplaced means?

Ever put it in a safe place and then forget where the safe place is?

Ever wonder how many strangers dislike you because of how someone else described you to them?

My silence does not mean I agree with you. It means your level of idiocy has rendered me speechless.

Does it count as saving a life if you refrain from killing them?

Apparently rock bottom has a basement.

Nothing ruins a Friday more than an understanding that today is Tuesday.

Ever had a day when you are holding a stick and everyone looks like a piñata?

Being an adult is mostly being exhausted, wishing you hadn't made plans and wondering how you hurt your back.

Ever get angry when you find a parking space and there's already a motorcycle parked in it?

Ever wonder what happened to the people who asked you for directions?

Sometimes you have to tell yourself it just wouldn't be worth the jail time.

The best feeling is waking up in the middle of the night and realising you still have hours to sleep.

This isn't life in the fast lane, it's life in the oncoming traffic.

Didn't see anyone important today so I'll wear the same clothes tomorrow.

Should you get compensated for every popcorn kernel that doesn't pop in every bag of popcorn?

There’s no excuse for laziness, but if you find one, let me know.

The human body is 80% water - so are cucumbers.

Procrastinate today. Tomorrow may be too late.

He’d even steal flies from a blind spider.

Volleyball is just a more intense version of "don't let the balloon touch the floor".

It would be wonderful if his brain would autocorrect words before they leave his mouth.

He's lowered his expectations to the point where they've already been met. Smart and efficient.

If you were half as funny as you think you are, you'd be twice as funny as you are now.

How can you look important when walking around a clipboard factory?

She gave me that strange look when I asked for her email number.

One can speak with a twang and still not say a thang.

If you are not willing to risk the unusual, you will have to settle for the ordinary. (Jim Rohn)

I'm sorry, in order for you to insult me I have to value your opinion. Nice try though.

If only closed minds came with closed mouths.

Journalism consists in buying white paper at two cents a kilo and selling it at fifty cents a kilo.

No one really listens to anyone else, and if you try it for a while you'll see why.

It's true that ninety-two percent of the stuff told you in confidence you couldn't get anyone else to listen to.

Talking to a golf ball won't do you any good, unless you do it while your opponent is teeing off.

If they gave out awards for laziness, she would send somebody to accept it for her.

I get ignored so much that my nickname should be Terms and Conditions.

The workshop on procrastination has been cancelled because no one got around to enrolling.

Anyone can be spontaneous if they have enough time to prepare for it.

Constantly losing socks in the laundry but finding change, so logically there has to be a sock fairy.

The number of times I think "I don't care" while people are speaking to me is getting out of hand.

Favourite poem is the one that starts, "Thirty days hath September," because unlike most poetry it actually tells you something. (Groucho Marx)

Just finished washing a load of paper plates if anyone's wondering about my bank account balance.

A lifetime of fire drills has prepared us to completely ignore the alarm during a real fire.

Life's disappointments are harder to take when you don't know any swear words.

We are here on earth to do good unto others. What the others are here for, I have no idea.

"Heartless" is a label that is all too often wrongly given to someone who is rational by someone who is emotional.

I'd like to cancel my subscription to 2021. I've tried the free trial and I'm not interested.

Note to self, don't introduce yourself to the new neighbours until they have all the heavy stuff moved in.

Don't ever put *just* the toilet seat down; the lid goes down with it - if you've got to work, so does she.

People better watch their P's and Q's before I start handing out F's and U's.

Now that I'm retired, I've taken up meditation. It beats sitting around doing nothing.

Scientists have proven that anything can sound impressive if you say scientists have proven it.

Most people say they are in favour of free speech until you say something they don't like.

Could the mattress and rug stores please tell us when they are *not* having a sale?

When the optimist falls into a pile of horse shit, he starts looking for the pony.

Nothing makes it easier to resist temptation than a proper bringing-up, a sound set of values - and witnesses.

Wear a smile and you have friends, wear a scowl and you have wrinkles.

Try to learn something about everything and everything about something. (Aldous Huxley)

They say the best things take time, that's why I'm always late.

Expensive clothing is usually a poor man's attempt to appear prosperous.

Most people believe most of the things they believe only because they believe that most people believe them.

A newspaper is just an oversized book with adverts and an expiry date.

Reality is what people who lack vision see.

You've made it when your friends tell their friends that you are their friend.

We seldom learn much from someone with whom we agree.

Does it bother anyone else when you hear someone say, "I arxed him"?

Fun activity: fire up your leaf blower and blow your neighbour's Chihuahua down the street.

Ever wish your teeth were as white as your legs?

Has anyone ever managed to finish a bottle of shampoo and a bottle of conditioner at the same time? No, I thought not.

After realising that her arts degree was useless she scanned the internet correcting dopey people's grammar.

Any poet who reads their verse in public may have other nasty habits.

Tolerance is just another word for indifference.

Obscenity is whatever happens to shock some elderly and ignorant magistrate. (Bertrand Russel)

Progress can just mean bad things happen faster.

Your chances of dying on the way to buying a lotto ticket are greater than your chances of winning.

Have you ever looked at the last load of washing and considered just throwing it away?

It is amazing how many problems you can solve by ignoring them.

Turns out I'm not an afternoon person either.

Parenting without a sense of humour is like being an accountant who is crap at maths.

Let us live so that when we come to die even the undertaker will be sorry. (Mark Twain)

The key to happiness is a lousy memory.

It currently feels like we're living in the "Days Leading Up To ..." section of the history books.

If at first you don't succeed, blame someone else and seek counselling.

What does "reading comprehension" even mean?

The three unwritten rules of life: 1 ... 2 ... 3 ...

May you have an idea you know is absolutely right but be unable to convince anyone. (Chinese curse)

Like me you know right from wrong. Wrong is the fun one.

If it's the thought that counts he should probably be in jail.

Trust me. Somewhere out there is a person younger than you who looks older than you.

Randomly wave at random people and for the rest of the day they'll wonder who you were.

Take care of your thoughts when you are alone and take care of your word when you are with people.

Leave your body to science because even scientists need a good laugh now and then.

Just because it is a bad idea doesn't mean it's not going to be a good time.

From a procrastination standpoint, today has been wildly successful.

It's easy to identify people who can't count to ten as they're in front of you in the supermarket express lane.

Immature is a word boring people use to describe fun people.

Friday the 13th is better than Monday the whatever.

Saying "with all due respect" lends gravitas to the massive pile of disrespect you're about to lay down.

Nobody ever, ever has gotten in or out of a hammock with dignity intact.

The first five days after the weekend are the hardest.

A great super power would be to delete my number from some other people's phone.

If it doesn't open, it's probably not your door.

Funny, I don't remember being absent-minded. Funny, I don't remember being absent-minded.

Those who live in the past often die in the present.

When I'm finally holding all the right cards, everyone wants to play chess.

Advertising is the art of making whole lies out of half truths.

Can anyone tell me what's offensive today? It's hard to keep up.

He was a man of his word ... and that word was "unreliable".

One nice thing about telling a clean joke is there's a good chance no one's heard it before.

Getting really tired of my neighbour's crappy wi-fi.

When you hear music coming out of your printer it will be the paper jamming again.

"Let me check my calendar" is the adult version of "Let me ask my mum."

Be good and you will be lonely. (Mark Twain)

Everyone is a damn fool for at least five minutes a day; wisdom consists of not exceeding the limit.

Organised people are just too lazy to look for things.

There are worse things than getting a call for a wrong number at 4 am - for example, it could be the right number.

Celebrate. Today is the furthest in history anyone has ever gone and you are part of it.

If some people said what's on their minds, they'd be speechless.

Life was much simpler when we could play a friendly game of Red Rover and just clothesline the people we didn't like.

The best thing about the future is that it comes one day at a time. (Abraham Lincoln)

If at first you don't succeed, we have a lot in common.

He tried to organise a hide-and-seek tournament, but it was a complete failure. Good players are hard to find.

The thing to do with a silly remark is to fail to hear it.

He wanted to meet again but I told him I don't water dead flowers.

Life is better with a dirty imagination.

It takes a real talent to be able to apologise in a manner that makes the offended person feel guilty.

People with narrow minds usually have broad tongues.

Any fool can criticise, condemn, and complain - and most fools do. (Dale Carnegie)

The best way to entertain some folks is to listen to them.

Most people tire of a lecture in ten minutes; clever people can do it in five; sensible people never go to lectures at all. (Stephen Leacock)

Keeping both feet firmly on the ground means you'll have trouble putting on your pants.

I may have a vacuum between my ears, but at least it's better than nothing.

Have you noticed that the most difficult light bulb to replace burns out first and most frequently.

Experience is the name everyone gives to their failures. (Oscar Wilde)

Jet planes long ago passed the speed of sound, and are fast approaching the speed of gossip.

Flatterers look like friends as wolves look like dogs.

We all have that one friend who needs to learn how to whisper.

Before Twitter we had no way of knowing the illiteracy rates of celebrities.

Auctioneers are proof white guys can rap if they try hard enough.

Apparently typos only become visible to the human eye after you hit send.

If you wonder what people used to do or how they lived their lives without the internet, ask Google.

Some people say I have a short temper, but I prefer to call it a swift and assertive reaction to bullshit.

Uncertainty makes people anxious, and anxiety is related to magical thinking.

The difficulty lies not so much in developing new ideas as in escaping from old ones.

There's nothing wrong with perfectionism.

It's that time of year to find out what your friends with pools have been up to since last summer.

The nice thing about egotists is they don't talk about other people. (George Carlin)

The world is ending in sixteen days and I still don't know what I'm going to wear.

Memories should be like text messages so we can delete the ones we don't like and keep the special ones forever.

I'm not an arrogant geek, I just understand things you can't begin to comprehend.

In the long run the pessimist may be proved right, but the optimist has a better time on the trip.

Life is like riding a bicycle. To keep your balance you must keep moving. (Albert Einstein)

If the police arrest a mime, do they tell him he has the right to remain silent?

The person who came up with the phrase "some assembly required" never tried to assemble anything.

Intelligent conversationalists are those who nod in agreement while you're talking.

Do female suicide bombers also get virgins?

One shouldn't say bad things about the illiterate - one should write them.

At no time is freedom of speech more precious than when a man hits his thumb with a hammer.

One problem with auto-correct is that you always end up posting some thong you didn't Nintendo.

It's sad that many people say they want justice when what they really want is revenge.

He has turned almost alarmingly blond - he's gone past platinum; he must be plutonium.

There is nothing so unbecoming on the beach as a wet kilt.

Don't take criticism from those you would not go to for advice.

For me dying is a lot like going camping. I don't want to do it.

He has left his body to science ... and science is contesting the will. (David Frost)

Go ask a little kid what a VCR is. I dare you.

He had just about enough intelligence to open his mouth when he wanted to eat, but certainly no more. (PG Wodehouse)

You are not young enough to know everything.

Technology is anything invented after you were born.

Experience is something you don't get until just after you need it.

Tolerance is that uncomfortable feeling that the other fellow might be right after all.

Praise does wonders for our sense of hearing.

A New Year's resolution is something that goes in one year and out the other.

Guards on the tomb of the unknown soldier do not wear rank badges so as not to outrank any of the unknown soldiers.

While on a ladder, never step back to admire your work.

A man with a beard, moustache and glasses has taken every precaution to avoid people doodling on photographs of him.

In the end a pessimist is either pleasantly surprised or has the satisfaction of knowing they were right all along.

If someone ever tells you "we need to talk" they don't care about anything you have to say.

Anyone with your IQ should have a low voice too.

The bigger the mouth, the better it looks shut.

When life hands you lemons, take them. Free stuff is good.

Dear life, when I asked "can life get any worse" it was a rhetorical question, not a challenge.

If they can make penicillin out of mouldy bread, they can sure make something out of you. (Muhammad Ali)

The floor is your home's biggest shelf.

Sometimes the thoughts in my head go for a stroll through my mouth and this is rarely a good thing.

Hang on to your youthful enthusiasms - you'll be able to use them better when you're older. (Seneca)

That group of mimes are capable of unspeakable things.

To see features on your TV that you never knew existed let a baby play with the remote for about twelve seconds.

Nothing spoils a good rant more than someone trying to spoil it with facts and reason.

With great power comes great electricity bill.

Dear advertising agencies, whoever told you we like loud TV ads lied.

I hear and I forget. I see and I remember. I do and I understand.

Remember the greener grass on the other side of the fence may be due to septic tank issues.

The sculptor Rodin said he just chose a block of marble and chopped off whatever he didn't need.

Art is making something out of nothing and selling it. (Frank Zappa)

Always do what you cannot do so you can learn how to do it.

Be thankful for the mess to clean after a party because it means you have been surrounded by friends.

Efficiency is a highly developed form of laziness.

Sorry I can't attend. My uncle's cousin's sister-in-law's best friend's insurance agent's roommate's pet goldfish died. Maybe next time.

If you listen very carefully, you can hear Monday sharpening its claws.

You're so clever hacker, here's my password ●●●●●●●●●●●●● .

Wish you could collect all the wonderful things people are giving up for Lent?

Lead me not into temptation - I can find the way myself.

Most people would like to be delivered from temptation but would like it to keep in touch. (Robert Orben)

It's not that I'm a laid-back person, it's just that I'm driven by a passionate, all-consuming desire to take it easy.

Nothing will dispel enthusiasm like a small admission fee.

Could crop circles be the work of a cereal killer?

Don't sell the skin until you have caught the roo.

If you're not living on the edge, you're taking up too much room.

If at first you don't succeed, look in the rubbish bin for the instructions.

Never put off until tomorrow what you can do the day after tomorrow. (Mark Twain)

The best things in life are actually really expensive.

You must learn from the mistakes of others. You can't possibly live long enough to make them all yourself.

Everyone is gifted, but not everyone opens their present.

The tragedy of life is not that it ends so soon, but that we wait so long to begin it.

I have a strong will but a weak won't.

This website may not be idiot proof, but at least it's dimwit resistant.

It's time for a new holiday, where people can recycle gifts they don't want.

Truism: the number of bracelets you can have depends entirely on the length of your arms.

You know you're working class when your TV is bigger than your book case.

Remember when men were polite and considerate and ladies expected them to be?

I'm sure wherever my dad is, he's looking down on us. He's not dead, just very condescending.

Fishing is a delusion entirely surrounded by liars in old clothes.

Take the last two digits of the year you were born plus the age you will be this year and it will equal 111. Check it out you disbelievers.

How would you feel when a zombie is looking for brains and it walks right past you?

Creativity is contagious. Pass it on. (Albert Einstein)

Never sure if you have free time or are just forgetting stuff?

Put glitter on top of all your friends' ceiling fans' blades. Wait till summer. Enjoy!

Ever want to put an "out of order" sticker on your forehead and call it a day?

A hobby is something you do to have fun whether you enjoy it or not.

Playing poker is as elaborate a waste of human intelligence as you could find outside an advertising agency.

Waiting for the day to see a judge take the verdict slip from the jury, look at it, and then turn and say, "Are you shittin' me?!"

It takes patience to listen. It takes skill to pretend you're listening.

Ever noticed the cigarette smoke always drifts in the direction of the non-smoker regardless of the direction of the breeze?

Joined Gamblers Anonymous; they gave me two to one I wouldn't make it.

Police never say thankyou for us committing crimes and thus keeping them employed.

Rembrandt painted seven hundred pictures; of these, three thousand are still in existence.

Pedantic? He is the type of person who would criticise a misspelling in a suicide note.

You can’t learn too soon that the most useful thing about a principle is that it can always be sacrificed to expediency.

In the interests of good taste, wish the bloke in line in front of me would pull his jeans up.

Knowledge has never been known to enter a head through an open mouth.

Criticism is not nearly as effective as sabotage.

Ever carried ten overloaded plastic bags in each hand rather than taking two trips to bring your groceries in?

Education can be the path from cocky ignorance to miserable uncertainty.

Of all the things you wear, your expression is most important.

Don't let your mind wander - it's too little to be let out alone.

Learn from Pandora's mistake - think outside the box.

You don't realise what you have until it is gone. Toilet paper is a good example.

Sneezed into the computer and an antivirus popped up.

If Facebook teaches us anything it is that not many people are ready for a spelling bee.

Remember when the library used to be your internet?

Opportunity is missed by most people because it is dressed in overalls and looks like work. (Thomas Edison)

Somedays I feel like running away, then I remember how much I hate running.

It's only embarrassing if you care what people think.

Border wall completed 2021. Headline: Mexico takes Gold, Silver & Bronze in pole vault at the Summer Olympics.

Wish people in this world would put as much effort into earning respect as they do demanding it.

Lazy is such an ugly word; let's call it selective participation.

No, a stress ball is not a ball to throw at people who stress you out.

Being an open book isn't helpful if you surround yourself with a bunch of illiterates.

You don't know what you've got until you lose it, but, then again, you don't know what you've been missing until it arrives.

For those who say patience is a virtue, try surfing the web with slow internet speed.

As your best friend I will always pick you up when you fall, after I have finished laughing.

They said he acted like he didn't care. He wasn't acting.

Whenever possible, please say whatever you have to say during commercials.

Remember back when we were kids and every time it was above 35 C outside they closed school? Me neither.

An empty web browsing history is a sure sign of guilt.

As you get older you will be less surprised if a random body part just falls off one day.

Most of us could be a morning person if morning was sometime around noon.

I'm great at remembering names. I just don't remember which one's yours.

Life is too short to waste it on getting mad at idiots.

Love that moment when you're cutting wrapping paper and the scissors start to glide.

The irony of all this is, the internet was created to save us time.

Today, I found out that "Made in China" stickers are made in Korea.

Nothing's more satisfying than when "the one that got away" turns into "whew, dodged that bullet."

The washing machine has seen me naked more often than anyone else.

Stopped understanding maths when the alphabet got involved.

Bought a packet of bird seed and wondered how long does it take for birds to grow once I plant them.

A zoo is a pleasant and instructive wildlife park, lately denounced for depriving animals of their right to starve or be eaten alive in their natural habitats.

Compromise is a deal in which two people get what neither of them wanted.

After-dinner speakers are often people who only have a few words to say, but seldom stop when they have said them.

With prcatsie you cna tpye 200 wrods a minuet liek me.

If scientists invented the legal system, eye-witness testimony would be inadmissible evidence.

Karate is the ancient Japanese art of getting people to buy lots of belts.

Underwear is an article of clothing which, when kept clean, ensures the wearer will never have an accident.

Advertising makes you think you've longed all your life for something you never even heard of.

Shhh ... don't tell the second place getter they are the first loser.

It could be worse. Spiders could have wings.

Secret: what we tell everybody to tell nobody. (Ambrose Bierce)

Think like a proton and stay positive.

Every journalist has a novel in them, which is an excellent place for it.

Did my first cartwheel the other day after thirty-five years. Thought it was like riding a bike. It's not.

If you think about getting a tattoo just decide to yell "look at me!" everywhere you go instead.

"Some assembly required" is IKEA for: "Here's a pine tree and some nails."

Note that fashion is something that goes out of style as soon as most people have one.

His office looked like his filing cabinets had sneezed.

Ever look at someone and think, "Why has no one hit you with a shovel yet?"

We used to have village idiots, but with the internet the bastards have gone global.

Mirrors don't lie, and, lucky for some of us, they don't laugh.

Listen, moron, if you're going to try and insult me, at least be grammatically correct. I'm too busy mentally correcting your errors to be offended.

Courage doesn't always roar; sometimes it's the quiet voice at the end of the day whispering, "I will try again tomorrow."

Remember when apparently the worst thing life could hand you was lemons?

If people couldn't profit from war there would be no war.

Consider this: a modern depression is a period during which we have to get along without the things our grandparents never dreamed of.

Nostalgia? How long's that been around? (Bill Bailey)

Ever thought that temptation is something which, when resisted, gives happiness and which, when yielded to, gives even greater happiness!

News is the same thing happening today that happened yesterday, but to different people.

Algebra is that branch of mathematics that is so scary it causes everybody to stop studying mathematics.

Jumping to conclusions is not half as much exercise as digging for facts.

Conscience doesn't keep you from doing anything - just keeps you from enjoying it.

If you believe the competitive spirit is dead, you haven't been in the supermarket when the cashier opens another checkout line.

Advice for pretty much anything that's broken is try and jiggle it.

Camping out is nature's way of feeding mosquitoes.

Miracle: an event described by those to whom it was told by men who did not see it. (Elbert Hubbard)

A second chance doesn't mean anything if nothing has been learned from the first mistake.

Insurance is just a form of gambling in which we bet on our chance of escaping disaster, and win only when we lose.

Weird how "news" and "fact checking" are treated like two separate concepts these days.

For fast-acting relief try slowing down. (Lily Tomlin)

Savages are people who don't know what is wrong until missionaries show them.

My anger management class pisses me off.

A hole-in-one occurs when a ball is hit directly from the tee into the hole in a single shot by a golfer who is always playing alone.

Etc. is a widely used device to make others believe that you know more than you actually do.

Bachelors believe in life, liberty, and the happiness of pursuit.

Success always occurs in private, and failure in full view.

Don't ever stand up to be counted or someone will take your seat.

Curiosity is the most powerful thing you own.

When putting things back together again, there will always be at least one piece left over that will not fit anywhere.

If you have only one nail, it will bend.

The sooner you fall behind, the more time you will have to catch up.

Creativity is great but plagiarism is faster.

If the supplier has it in stock it didn't need replacing in the first place.

If you don't say it, they can't repeat it.

I don't run for fun! If you see me running past you, you better start running too because something is coming.

Have you ever noticed that the uglier a man's legs are, the better he plays golf?

The worst golf shots always occur when playing with someone you are trying to impress.

Nothing travels faster than the speed of light, with the possible exception of bad news, which obeys its own set of laws. (Douglas Adams)

There are never enough hours in a day, but always too many days before Saturday.

Microwaves have two settings - cold in the centre and surface of the sun.

How many Snickers are an acceptable meal replacement?

Future generations with all-digital textbooks will look back and laugh at us for having to carry 25 kg backpacks in high school.

Anyone else starting to feel bullied by all the anti-bullying news items?

If we knew what we were doing, it wouldn't be called research. (Albert Einstein)

Does anyone else watch dead bodies in the movies to catch them breathing?

If you want a quiet work place get a job in the complaint department at a parachute packing plant.

To locate the slow-moving traffic lane or supermarket check-out lane, get in it.

It is usually accepted that history doesn't repeat itself - historians merely repeat each other.

Brute force, clumsiness, ignorance, and superstition will always triumph over science, skill, knowledge, and logic.

The day you buy your boat regardless of how big it is, it will be one metre too short.

One good thing about apathy is you don't have to exert yourself to show you're sincere about it.

The courthouse is a really great place to see people with neck tattoos wearing ties.

Hide all your porn on VHS - no one will ever find it.

Why don't you get a haircut? You look like a chrysanthemum? (P G Wodehouse)

All photographers are aware that the best shots are generally attempted through the lens cap.

When the water reaches the upper deck, follow the rats.

If you like to fall asleep in bed but wake up on the floor, owning satin sheets might not be for you.

The chance of forgetting something is directly proportional to … to …

When the waiter says "Table for two" I always like to look surprised and whisper, "You can see him too?"

Remember recording a song onto tape from the radio while hoping the DJ didn't talk over the song?

Dear lady driver in front of me, it is a speed bump, not a bloody land mine.

There is no more frightening experience than seeing a police car make a U-turn behind you.

Those who know the least will always know it the loudest.

If some people listened to themselves more often, they'd talk less.

Experience: what you get from being inexperienced.

If I was doing any better, I'd have to hire somebody to help me enjoy it.

People today have more time-saving devices yet less time. How come?

Don't be fooled, antique shops are simply a junk store that has raised its prices.

If you ask me, every Friday is a Good Friday.

Imagine how creepy the first guy to dress up as a clown must have been. Where in hell did he get that idea?

All I heard was, "I swear this will be really funny" ... then we were in jail.

If you don't take care of your customer, your competitor will.

He is at his wit's end - it is true that he had not far to go. (Lord Byron)

When his daughter plays the violin, it sounds as if the strings are still in the cat.

Ever wonder how many chameleons could have sneaked onto the Ark?

What you don't see with your eyes, don't invent with your mouth.

A gift card is the polite way to say here's $50; go and get your own damn gift.

Why is it that an article about errors will contain errors?

Why is it that a small boy with a hammer finds that everything he encounters needs pounding, but girls not so much?

She seemed to have a theological halo around her head as she ambled towards him with that peculiarly sexy way of walking which was really due to an old spinal injury and incipient arthritis.

Why choose to write and why especially about humour?

Some answers to the question ...

Every time you find humour in a difficult situation, you win.

Always laugh when you can. It is cheap medicine. (Lord Byron)

Wit is the sudden marriage of ideas which, before their union, were not perceived to have any relation. (Mark Twain)

Writer's block is a fancy term made up by whiners so they can have an excuse to drink alcohol.

Humour is a spontaneous, wonderful bit of an outburst that just comes. It's unbridled, it's unplanned, it's full of surprises. (Erma Bombeck)

Humour is a serious thing. It is one of our greatest natural resources which must be preserved at all costs.

When you lose one sense other senses are enhanced, that's why if you lose your sense of humour your sense of misery is enhanced.

There's a hell of a distance between wise-cracking and wit. Wit has truth in it; wise-cracking is simply calisthenics with words. (Dorothy Parker)

People with a good sense of humour have a better sense of life.

We need a GPS app to help some people find their sense of humour. And you know some of them.

Next to being witty, the best thing is being able to quote another's wit.

Any joke is a one-liner if the notebook you write it in is wide enough.

If you get offended by any one liners in this book, feel free to Tweet your outrage on a mobile phone made by a ten-year-old in China.

Blessed are those who can laugh at themselves; they will never cease to be amused.

On Writing

Failures are built into the process of writing. The wastebasket has evolved for a reason. (Margaret Atwood)

There is nothing to writing. All you do is sit down at a keyboard and bleed.

Plagiarism is the fear of a blank page.

First drafts don't have to be perfect, they just have to be written.

There is no way to stop. Writers go on writing long after it becomes financially unnecessary because it hurts less to write than it does not to write.

Is writing a socially acceptable form of schizophrenia?

I hate writing; I love having written. (Dorothy Parker)

(And Amen to that - *RP*)

Trust you enjoyed spending time browsing through the book, enjoying it alone or sharing with friends. If others would like a copy of any of the four One Liner books, contact rprince@ozemail.com.au

Life is so much easier with a sense of humour. Thanks for your company along the way. ***Ray Prince***

www.ingramcontent.com/pod-product-compliance
Lightning Source LLC
Chambersburg PA
CBHW071552030726
47593CB00001BA/121

* 9 7 8 0 9 9 2 3 8 4 9 5 1 *